OECD HEALTH DATA 2004
A COMPARATIVE ANALYSIS OF 30 COUNTRIES

ECO–SANTÉ OCDE 2004
ANALYSE COMPARATIVE DE 30 PAYS

OECD GESUNDHEITSDATEN 2004
VERGLEICHENDE ANALYSE VON 30 LÄNDERN

ECO–SALUD OCDE 2004
ANÁLISIS COMPARATIVO DE 30 PAÍSES

User's Guide
Guide de l'utilisateur
Benutzerhandbuch
Guía de utilización

English

TABLE OF CONTENTS

TABLE DES MATIÈRES

Français

INHALTSVERZEICHNIS

CONTENIDO

Deutch

Español

OECD HEALTH DATA 2004
A COMPARATIVE ANALYSIS OF 30 COUNTRIES

User's Guide

OECD HEALTH DATA 2004 was developed jointly by the OECD Secretariat and IRDES (Institut de Recherche et d'Etude en Economie de la Santé), a French research institute specialised in health economics and health statistics.

The OECD Health Data 2004 team comprised Gaëlle Balestat, Marie-Clémence Canaud, Manfred Huber, Gaetan Lafortune, David Morgan, and Eva Orosz. The IRDES team comprised Catherine Banchereau, Martine Broïdo, Jacques Harrouin, Christophe Lainé, Florence Naudin, and Thierry Rochereau.

For any questions regarding data, and sources and methods, please contact:	For technical support, please contact:
OECD Health Policy Unit 2, rue André Pascal F-75775 Paris Cedex 16 (France) Fax : (33) 1 44 30 63 61 E-mail : health.contact@oecd.org	IRDES 10, rue Vauvenargues F-75018 Paris (France) Fax : (33) 1 53 93 43 50 (please ask for the Eco-Santé team) E-mail : ecosante@irdes.fr Web : www.irdes.fr

Frequently Asked Questions

OECD and IRDES maintain Internet sites where you will find responses to Frequently Asked Questions, as well as information about data updates and variables, sample tables, and the expected publication date of OECD Health Data 2005.
- For technical problems, consult: www.irdes.fr/ecosante/faq.htm
- For information and data updates, consult: www.oecd.org/health/healthdata/
and click on [Frequently Asked Questions] from the OECD Health Data page.

Information on OECD Health Data 2004 on the Internet

- www.oecd.org/health/healthdata/
- www.irdes.fr/ecosante/index.htm

The OECD Health Data 2004 package consists of:
- A CD-ROM containing the programme files, data files and utilities.
- This User's Guide.

FOREWORD

After more than fifteen years of collecting statistical series, the OECD has completed thirteen editions of its electronic database on health systems.

The 2004 edition includes new data together with an enhanced software. The standard definitions of variables and the corresponding documentation of country-specific sources and methods have been revised and expanded. Thanks to the contributions of the original suppliers of the data, these files constitute a very rich tool for understanding the trends or levels of the series. For the Windows 98/2000/NT/Me/XP environment, various *OECD Health Data* functions have been revised and improvements have been made to this user-friendly software which enjoys the esteem of thousands of users.

Grateful acknowledgement is given for the financial support of the Centers for Medicare and Medicaid Services (CMS, formerly HCFA) of the United States Department of Health and Human Resources. Warm thanks are also due to the hundreds of statisticians in the 30 Member countries who have produced the data and qualitative information on which the data file is based.

INTRODUCTION

OECD Health Data 2004 is an interactive database comprising data on a range of key aspects of the health care systems in the 30 OECD Member countries which are presented in a demographic, economic and social context.

The latest version, is a fast, userfriendly package that enables PC users to query OECD data files and analyse them using tables, charts and maps. It also offers the option of exporting data to other software packages. Users can select the variables, countries and years they want. The data, comprising some 1 200 different series, span the period 1960-2002, with selected longtime series from 1960 onwards. Most data cover the 1980s and 1990s, many of which continue up to 2001 or 2002, with selected Secretariat estimates for 2003.

OECD Health Data 2004 is a quadrilingual product (English/French/German/Spanish) under Windows 98/2000/NT/Me/XP. It was developed jointly by OECD and IRDES and is the result of their combined experience in related fields:

- The publication and updating of statistical indicators on health and economic policies in 30 countries;
- The development of a macroeconomic database to describe how a health system works.

This User's Guide provides information on the contents of the database, the analysis functions it offers, and practical instructions on how to use the programme.

NEW FEATURES IN THE 2004 VERSION OF *OECD HEALTH DATA*

OECD Health Data 2004 offers a range of new features and improvements:

- New installation procedure;
- New design of the application to follow XP-style;
- Search features by key words and full text added in the hypertext for *Sources and Methods*, along with a new navigation index;
- Software and list of variables available in Russian;
- Upgraded tools to change the language of the software (one click provides all features in the same language);
- Preliminary results from the OECD Health Project included in the hypertext.

Last minute modifications to *OECD Health Data 2004* are presented in the ReadMe.txt file. This file can be consulted at the end of the installation procedure. To read it later, simply click on the ReadMe icon in *OECD Health Data 2004*.

CHAPTER ONE: INSTALLING *OECD HEALTH DATA 2004*

Minimum hardware characteristics and system configuration

To use this software you need:

- Windows 98/2000/NT/Me/XP;
- 64 MB RAM;
- Free hard disk space of 70 MB;
- A CD-ROM drive (the CD-ROM will be used only during the installation procedure);
- Graphic card: 16 bits 800x600.

If you have an earlier version of **OECD Health Data** on your hard disk, you are advised to delete it, so as not to waste space on your hard disk. To do so, select the icon Add/Remove programs in the Control Panel. Please note that your personal library of pre-defined tables cannot be transferred from previous versions of *OECD Health Data*.

Installing *OECD Health Data 2004*

Please note that before installing the software you should close all applications and disable the anti-virus installation you might have on your computer. You should also make sure that you have the rights to install software onto the location you choose, or consult your PC/network administrator.

To install the software, start Windows and insert the CD-ROM into the drive. Installation on a network is detailed in a box below.

The CD-ROM will be used only during the installation procedure.

Click **[Start]**, then "Run"
On the [Open] line, type "d:\install" where d is your CD-ROM drive.
Click [OK] to confirm your choice.

When your CD-ROM drive is configured for "AutoBoot", the installation of **OECD Health Data 2004** starts automatically as soon as the disk is inserted into the drive.

The installation proceeds in five stages:

- Select the language desired for installation: English, French, German, Spanish;
- The user must accept the copyright contract of the software;
- Enter the information concerning the user as well as **the serial number of the CD-ROM, which appears on the inside cover** of this User's guide. When the number is correct the installation procedure continues, otherwise an error message appears and the number has to be entered again;
- Choose the directory where you would like to install the software. The programme checks if there is sufficient space available on the hard disk. If not, you should free some disk space or change the destination directory;
- The last window asks the user to confirm choices. Installation of the system files follows automatically.

At the end of the installation procedure, a folder is created containing the icons necessary to run *OECD Health Data 2004*.

At the end of the installation procedure, a window pops up, providing useful contacts for questions on the software, as well as the OECD and IRDES Web addresses.

NB: Users may have to reboot their computer after installation, and will be notified by the program if this is the case

---

The installation of *OECD Health Data 2004* on a network

To install the software on a network, the network administrator has to first install the "network" part of the software on a network drive accessible to all potential users. This procedure is the same as the single-version installation (see above). The network administrator then has to install the "client" part on each workstation. To do so, the administrator launches the Install.exe programme, found in the sub-directory USER. For example, if you have installed the software on the drive E:\APPLI\ ECOSANTE2004, you should go to E:\APPLI\ECOSANTE2004\USER\INSTALL.EXE

> Installing the "client" part automatically leads to the creation of a folder c :\ecowin2004. If you wish to copy this local folder somewhere else, you will have to modify the parameters LocalPath in the file Ecowin.ini, located in the Windows folder.

The default option for work saved by each user is their local C:\ecowin2004\result directory. This local directory permits each user to save and access his/her own groups of countries and saved tables. The local installation occupies less than 1 MB on the user's hard drive.

Starting *OECD Health Data 2004*

Choose [Start-up Programmes *OECD Health Data 2004*] and position the pointer on [*OECD Health Data*].

At least 5 MB of free space are required after installation on your hard disk for the software to run correctly and store working and back-up files.

Once the software is running, you can try out different options, guided by the successive windows and referring to the information zones of the windows.

Screen tips — see below — are automatically activated when the software is first used. It is, however, recommended to read this Guide to learn more about the software before using it for the first time.

Uninstalling *OECD Health Data*

To uninstall *OECD Health Data 2004*, exit the application.

Click on the Start-up button and choose Settings. In the Control Panel, select the icon Add/Remove Programs. Select [*OECD Health Data 2004*] in the list and click on Add/Remove. Click OK to confirm the uninstallation of the program.

This erases all the *OECD Health Data 2004* files. You do not need the CD-ROM to uninstall the program.

Updating data files via Internet

Certain errors may be detected in the statistical series, or additional data may become available after the release of the software. It is highly recommended that you integrate these new values into your software by downloading them from the OECD or IRDES Internet sites.

On the Internet:

- Connect to one of these sites via the OECD or IRDES logos on the main menu:
  - ⇨ the OECD site: www.oecd.org/health/healthdata/;
  - ⇨ the IRDES site: www.irdes.fr/ecosante/index.htm;
- Click on the [Updates] button on the OECD site or on [Mise à jour des données] on the IRDES site;
- Double-click on [Download] ([Chargement]) and name the folder on the PC into which the files are to be downloaded.

Under Windows:

- Once the file is downloaded, double-click on the icon (or word) to start the installation;
- The file downloaded is a self-extracting (.EXE) file containing 2 files:
  - ⇨ the database update proper;
  - ⇨ a ReadMe file which lists the updates.
- Type in the name of the folder where you have installed your database *OECD Health Data 2004* (for instance c:\software\ecowin2004), and click on OK to confirm;
- A window appears as the updating process is about to start, displaying the title of the database and its version (for instance, *OECD Health Data 2004* 2nd edition.): click on « Start update» to launch the process.
- If the update does not start, please carefully check the name of the folder where the database has been installed and type it in again.

In the main window of OECD Health Data 2004:

Once the update is completed, the date and the name of the version under the title "*OECD HEALTH DATA 2004*" are modified.

CHAPTER TWO: QUERYING THE DATABASE

The *OECD Health Data 2004* main window

The different software functions are selected by clicking buttons. Clicking once either carries out a command immediately or leads you to a dialogue box in order to select various options before executing the command.

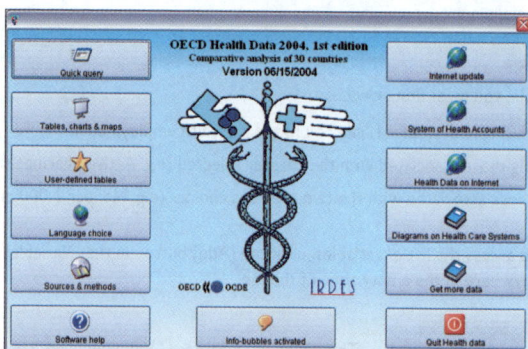

[Quick Query] is used to select a variable and retrieve the relevant data for one or all of the reference countries for one, two or all years available, and to calculate growth for the relevant period. This button can also be used to create maps, to print and to export a table.	**[Sources & methods]** gives access to the contents of Variable help, i.e. the attached definitions, sources and methods. Click **[Software help]** to access OECD Health Data help contents.
Click **[Tables, charts & maps]** to select one or more variables and obtain data for one or more countries for one or more years and to calculate the growth rate for the relevant period. This button can also be used to create charts and maps.	**[Info-bubbles activated]** activates or deactivates information on the nature and functions of software buttons.
Click on **[User-defined tables]** to retrieve a table previously created by you, or pre-defined by the Health Policy Unit. You can thus save your own library of tables.	**Direct Internet access**: buttons with this logo give you direct access to relevant OECD Health Web sites, including page for Internet updates download.
Click **[Language choice]** to select your working language for the software (English, French, German or Spanish) as well as for the help facility (English or French).	Click **[Quit Health Data]** to end your OECD Health Data session.

Help

Help with variables: Sources and Methods

The Sources and Methods attached to the variables are accessible either contextually or via a general index.

To access <u>context-sensitive help</u>, right-click an item to look up the standard definition, source and/or deviations. In *OECD Health Data 2004*, context-sensitive help is available from both the Chapter and Variable lists.

To access the general index for help on using variables, click the [Sources] button when it is available. Select the chapter and then the variable for which you require information.

Two other databases, produced by the IRDES, can be installed alongside *OECD Health Data 2004*:

Eco-Santé FRANCE and

Eco-Santé REGIONAL (France).

When at least two of these three databases have been installed, select the one desired from the scroll bar which is right in front of the active database. The logo screen indicates which database is active.

Creating tables, charts and maps

Selecting a variable

Before creating a table, you must first select:

- the Chapter, to which the desired variable belongs (e.g. Health employment);
- the Variable, among those associated with the chapter selected (e.g. Active pharmacists);
- the Unit, among those associated with the two previous choices (e.g. No. per 1 000 inhabitants).

To access the list of variables, click the [Add] button in the "Variables" window or click anywhere in the empty zone of the tab.

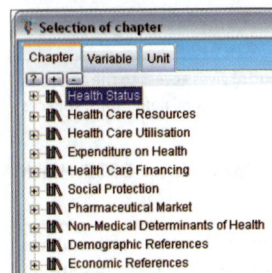

⇨ The titles of Chapters, Variables and Units are displayed in abbreviated form, but are sufficiently explicit to allow a selection.

⇨ They are listed in logical sequence so that you can easily locate the variable you want. You will also find a list of variables in Chapter 3 of this Guide.

There are three buttons on the "chapter" tab:

To display the full list of indicators (chapters, sub-chapters, variables), you must click on the [+]. Conversely, clicking on the [-] button of this tab reduces the detail provided at the lower level. [?] allows you to access software help.

Multiselection

There is another way to select variables common to several chapters. However, this procedure requires prior familiarity with the variables contained in these chapters.

Check the Multiselection box. Boxes appear in front of each chapter: check the boxes corresponding to the chapters containing the variables you wish to select.

Then click on the button [Next]. The next window displays the choice of variables common to the chapters you have just selected. To select the variables and then the units, follow the same procedure as before.

Selecting countries

To select a country, click the "Countries" tab.

The top left-hand box lists the 30 OECD Member countries; the bottom left-hand box lists the country groups. The right-hand box lists the countries or country groups selected.

Selecting one or more countries

To select a country:

- double-click the country name; or
- click the country name and the [+] button.

To select all the countries, click the [++] button. All the countries then appear in the right-hand box. To deselect one or all countries, click on the [-] or [--] button respectively.

Diagrams on Health Care Systems

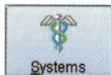

Systems

This facility which helps to better understand Health Care Systems is accessible either contextually or via a general index. It covers most of the OECD countries and consists of descriptive diagrams of the actors present on the health care "market" and their interrelationships. In some cases, two or more charts are included for one country, to show the evolution of the health care reforms in that country over the past decade or more. Contextual help is accessible through clicking the right mouse button on the country for which help is desired. To access the general index for Systems click on the **[Systems]** button. Select the country for which help is desired.

Selecting years and periods

To calculate growth rates, which require the prior selection of years and periods, click the "Years & Periods" tab.

The "Years available" box, on the left, lists the years for which data are available. However, since not all years have figures for each variable and all countries, click the [Availability] button in the bottom right-hand corner of the window to check the availability of data for your selected variable.

Blue buttons = years for which figures are available
Green buttons = years selected

Displaying the results

Before a table can be viewed, the warning below appears, regarding cross-country comparisons.

Click on OK to display the table.

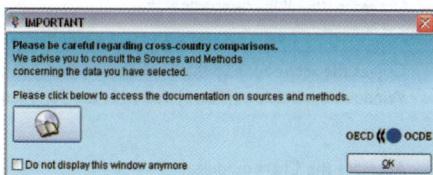

Table toolbar

The toolbar contains icons with the following functions:

  Minimises/maximises the toolbar.

  Reduces/increases the scale of the table displayed.

  Automatically adjusts the width of all the columns according to their content.

Sets all the columns at the same width as that of the active column.

Shows/hides gridlines.

Displays/closes the legend window.

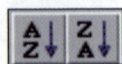

Sorts the elements of the table in ascending/descending order, on the basis of the active column.

Calculates the sum of the values in the active column. The result appears in the last line.

Deletes a column from the table. By default, this column number is the active column, but another can be specified by noting its rank.

Calculates a comparative index.

Adds a column providing ranking.

Calculates the arithmetic mean of the values in the active column. The result appears in the last line.

Accesses the table print set-up screen.

Accesses the table export screen.

Copies the active zone to the Clipboard so that it can be retrieved and pasted into another Windows application ([Paste] option in the Edit Menu or the [Ctrl-V] shortcut).

Accesses the Chart module.

Constructs a map based on the active column, when the rows of the table are countries.

Accesses software help.

Accesses variable help (Sources and Methods).

Exits the "View table" window.

To modify a column heading, double-click on the column. To modify the table title, double-click in the empty cell in the top left of the table.

These toolbar functionalities can be accessed directly by right-clicking on the title of a column in a table. Right-clicking on the title of an indicator (with variables in rows and years or countries in columns) brings up the definition, sources and methods for the selected indicator.

Exporting tables

The export parameters can be accessed from the toolbar in the "View" screen.

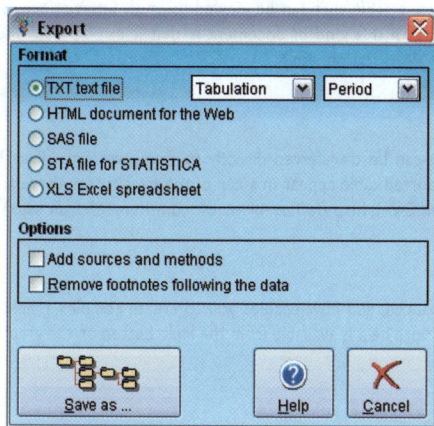

Five export formats are proposed:

● **Text.TXT**

This option creates an easy-to-use text file. You can choose the type of column separator (tab, space, comma, semi-colon) and the decimal symbol (point or comma).

● **SAS** System

The SAS System requires two files: a file containing the data (extension "DAT") and a file with the description of the variables and the breakdown of the data file (extension "SAS"). To import a file under SAS format, you have to run the program. From the data file, this generates a file in the temporary SAS (Work) directory. You can consult the result in the SAS environment (For further information on the SAS system: www.sas.com/).

Click the [Save As] button to select a path for saving the file. This opens a new window indicating by default the directory in which you are currently working.

You can then use normal Windows conventions to display the directories and to select the directory in which you wish to place your file.

Enter a name for your file on the "Name" line in this window. The default extension will be that of the export format you have chosen.

Click the [Save] button. A message is displayed on screen telling you that the file has been properly saved. Click the [Cancel] button to return to the "Export" window.

- **STA file for STATISTICA**

This format enables you to create a file with the extension .STA for the statistical software Statistica, made by StatSoft company (www.statsoft.com/). The title of the table, the data series and the labels of the variables appear in the file created.

- **HTML**

This format enables you to create a table that can be viewed using an Internet browser (ie Netscape or Internet Explorer). The advantage of this kind of document is that it can be displayed on most types of computers (PC, Macintosh, Unix Workstation, etc.).

- **Excel.XLS**

This option creates a file which can be transferred directly to Excel, version 4.0 or higher, without any conversion. The titles of the exported table appear in a cell of the Excel sheet above and to the left of the table. (For further information on Excel: http://office.microsoft.com/home/default.aspx).

Chart module

The chart module has been enhanced, and now enables you to create complex graphs, selecting the data directly from the table created. More help is available from the Help button on the graph.

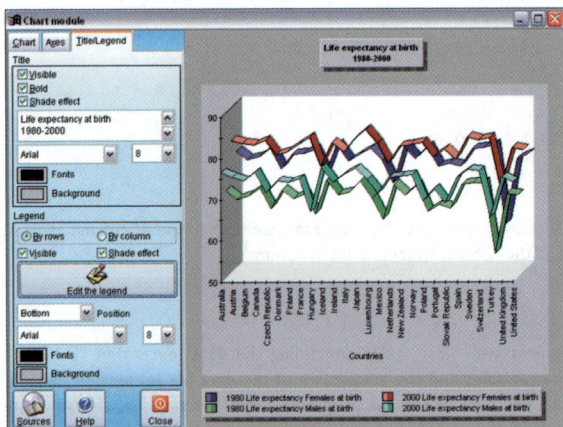

CHAPTER THREE: LIST OF VARIABLES IN THE 2004 EDITION

PART I - HEALTH STATUS

Mortality

Life expectancy
Females at birth
Females at age 40
Females at age 60
Females at age 65
Females at age 80
Males at birth
Males at age 40
Males at age 60
Males at age 65
Males at age 80
Total population at birth

Causes of mortality
All causes
Infectious and parasitic diseases
HIV disease
Malignant neoplasms
Malignant neoplasms of colon
Malignant neoplasms of lung
Malignant neoplasms of female breast
Malignant neoplasms of cervix
Malignant neoplasms of prostate
Diseases of blood
Endocrine, nutritional and metabolic diseases
Diabetes mellitus
Mental and behavioural disorders
Diseases of nervous system
Diseases of circulatory system
Ischaemic heart diseases
Acute myocardial infarction
Cerebrovascular diseases
Diseases of respiratory system
Influenza and pneumonia
Bronchitis, asthma and emphysema
Diseases of digestive system
Chronic liver diseases/cirrhosis
Diseases of skin and subcutaneous tissue
Diseases of musculoskeletal system

Diseases of genitourinary system
Complications of pregnancy/childbirth
Perinatal conditions
Congenital anomalies
Symptoms and ill-defined conditions
External causes
Land transport accidents
Accidental falls
Intentional self-harm
Assault
Adverse effects from medicines
Misadventures to patient during surgical/medi-
cal care

Maternal & infant mortality
Infant mortality
Neonatal mortality
Perinatal mortality
Maternal mortality

Potential years of life lost
All causes
Infectious and parasitic diseases
HIV disease
Malignant neoplasms
Malignant neoplasms of colon
Malignant neoplasms of lung
Malignant neoplasms of female breast
Malignant neoplasms of cervix
Malignant neoplasms of prostate
Diseases of blood
Endocrine, nutritional and metabolic diseases
Diabetes mellitus
Mental and behavioural disorders
Diseases of nervous system
Diseases of circulatory system
Ischaemic heart diseases
Acute myocardial infarction
Cerebrovascular diseases
Diseases of respiratory system
Influenza and pneumonia
Bronchitis, asthma and emphysema
Diseases of digestive system
Chronic liver diseases/cirrhosis

Diseases of skin and subcutaneous tissue
Diseases of musculoskeletal system
Diseases of genitourinary system
Complications of pregnancy/childbirth
Perinatal conditions
Congenital anomalies
Symptoms and ill-defined conditions
External causes
Land transport accidents
Accidental falls
Intentional self-harm
Assault
Adverse effects from medicines
Misadventures to patient during surgical/medical care

Morbidity

Perceived health status
Health ≥ good, female, 15-24
Health ≥ good, female, 25-44
Health ≥ good, female, 45-64
Health ≥ good, female, 65+
Health ≥ good, female, all ages
Health ≥ good, male, 15-24
Health ≥ good, male, 25-44
Health ≥ good, male, 45-64
Health ≥ good, male, 65+
Health ≥ good, male, all ages
Health ≥ good, total, 15-24
Health ≥ good, total, 25-44
Health ≥ good, total, 45-64
Health ≥ good, total, 65+
Health ≥ good, total, all ages

Infant health
Low birthweight

Congenital anomalies
Spina bifida
Transposition of great vessels
Limb reduction
Down's syndrome

Dental health
Decayed-missing-filled-teeth, DMFT

Communicable diseases
Acquired immunodeficiency syndrome (AIDS)

Cancer
Malignant neoplasms
Malignant neoplasms of colon
Malignant neoplasms of lung
Malignant neoplasms female breast
Malignant neoplasms of cervix
Malignant neoplasms of prostate

Injuries
Injuries in road traffic accidents

Absence from work due to illness
Self-reported absence from work due to illness
Compensated absence from work due to illness

PART 2 - HEALTH CARE RESOURCES

Health employment
Total health employment
Total hospital employment
Practising physicians
Female practising physicians
General practitioners
Practising specialists
Practising dentists
Practising pharmacists
Practising nurses

In-patient beds
Acute care beds
Long-term care beds

Employment-to-beds ratio
Acute care hospital staff ratio
Acute care nurses staff ratio

Medical technology
Computed Tomography Scanners
Magnetic Resonance Imaging Units
Radiation therapy equipment
Lithotriptors
Hemodialysis stations
Mammographs

Education in health and welfare
Health graduates, ISCED 3
Health graduates, ISCED 4
Health graduates, ISCED 5A

Health graduates, ISCED 5B

Health graduates, ISCED 6

PART 3 - HEALTH CARE UTILISATION

Prevention (Immunisation)

Immunisation: Diphteria, Tetanus, Pertussis

Immunisation: Measles

Immunisation: Influenza

Consultations

Doctors' consultations

Dentists' consultations

In-patient utilisation

Acute care beddays

Acute care occupancy rate

Acute care turnover rate

Average length of stay

Average Length of Stay: in-patient & acute care

Average length of stay: in-patient care

Average length of stay: acute care

Average length of stay by Diagnostic categories

All causes

Infectious and parasitic diseases

HIV disease

Malignant neoplasms

Malignant neoplasms of colon

Malignant neoplasms of lung

Malignant neoplasms female breast

Malignant neoplasms of prostate

Diseases of blood

Endocrine, nutritional and metabolic diseases

Diabetes mellitus

Diseases of nervous system

Senile cataract

Otitis media

Diseases of circulatory system

Ischaemic heart diseases

Acute myocardial infarction

Cerebrovascular diseases

Diseases of respiratory system

Influenza and pneumonia

Bronchitis, asthma and emphysema

Diseases of digestive system

Ulcers

Appendicitis

Inguinal and femoral hernia

Chronic liver diseases/cirrhosis

Cholelithiasis

Diseases of skin and subcutaneous tissue

Diseases of musculoskeletal system

Osteoarthrosis

Intevertebral disc disorders

Osteoporosis

Diseases of genitourinary system

Complications of pregnancy/childbirth

Normal delivery

Perinatal conditions

Congenital anomalies

Symptoms and ill-defined conditions

External causes

Fracture of neck of femur

All categories not elsewhere classified

Discharges

Discharge rates by Diagnostic categories

All causes

Infectious and parasitic diseases

HIV disease

Malignant neoplasms

Malignant neoplasms of colon

Malignant neoplasms of lung

Malignant neoplasms female breast

Malignant neoplasms of prostate

Diseases of blood

Endocrine, nutritional and metabolic diseases

Diabetes mellitus

Diseases of nervous system

Senile cataract

Otitis media

Diseases of circulatory system

Ischaemic heart diseases

Acute myocardial infarction

Cerebrovascular diseases

Diseases of respiratory system

Influenza and pneumonia

Bronchitis, asthma and emphysema

Diseases of digestive system

Ulcers
Appendicitis
Inguinal and femoral hernia
Chronic liver diseases/cirrhosis
Cholelithiasis
Diseases of skin and subcutaneous tissue
Diseases of musculoskeletal system
Osteoarthrosis
Intevertebral disc disorders
Osteoporosis
Diseases of genitourinary system
Complications of pregnancy/childbirth
Normal delivery
Perinatal conditions
Congenital anomalies
Symptoms and ill-defined conditions
External causes
Fracture of neck of femur
All categories not elsewhere classified

Surgical procedures

Total surgical procedures
All procedures (in-patient and day cases)
In-patient cases
Day cases

Surgical procedures by ICD-CM
Cataract surgery
Tonsillectomy with or without adenoidectomy
Percutaneous coronary interventions
Coronary stenting
Coronary bypass
Cardiac catheterisation
Pacemakers
Ligation and stripping of varicose veins
Appendectomy
Cholecystectomy
Laparoscopic cholecystectomy
Inguinal and femoral hernia
Prostatectomy (transurethral)
Prostatectomy (excluding transurethral)
Hysterectomy (vaginal only)
Caesarean section
Hip replacement
Knee replacement
Breast-conserving surgery
Mastectomy

Transplants and dialyses
Bone marrow transplant
Heart transplant
Liver transplant
Lung transplant
Kidney transplant
Functioning kidney transplants
End-stage renal failure patients
Patients undergoing dialysis
Patients undergoing home-dialysis

PART 4 - EXPENDITURE ON HEALTH

National expenditure on health

Total expenditure on health
Total expenditure on health
Total current expenditure on health
Total investment on medical facilities
Public expenditure on health
Public current expenditure on health
Public investment on medical facilities
Private expenditure on health
Private current expenditure on health
Private investment on medical facilities

Expenditure on personal health care
Total expenditure on personal health care
Public expenditure on personal health care
Private expenditure on personal health care

Expenditure on collective health care
Total expenditure on collective health care
Public expenditure on collective health care
Private expenditure on collective health care

Prevention and public health
Total expenditure on prevention and public health
Public expenditure on prevention and public health
Private expenditure on prevention and public health

Expenditure on health administration & insurance
Total expenditure on health administration and insurance
Public expenditure on health administration and insurance
Private expenditure on health administration and insurance

Expenditure on health-related functions

Expenditure on education and training of health personnel

Total expenditure on health R&D

Public expenditure on health R&D

Expenditure on medical services

Expenditure on medical services by functions

Total expenditure on medical services

Total expenditure on curative and rehabilitative care

Total expenditure on long-term nursing care

Total expenditure on ancillary services

Total expenditure on services not allocated by function

Public expenditure on medical services

Public expenditure on curative and rehabilitative care

Public expenditure on long-term nursing care

Public expenditure on ancillary services

Public expenditure on services not allocated by function

Private expenditure on medical services

Private expenditure on curative and rehabilitative care

Private expenditure on long-term nursing care

Private expenditure on ancillary services

Private expenditure on services not allocated by function

Expenditure on in-patient care

Total expenditure on in-patient care

Total expenditure on curative and rehabilitative in-patient care

Total expenditure on long-term nursing in-patient care

Public expenditure on in-patient care

Public expenditure on curative and rehabilitative in-patient care

Public expenditure on long-term nursing inpatient care

Private expenditure on in-patient care

Private expenditure on curative and rehabilitative in-patient care

Private expenditure on long-term nursing in-patient care

Expenditure on day care

Total expenditure on day care

Total expenditure on curative and rehabilitative day care

Total expenditure on long-term nursing daycare

Public expenditure on day care

Public expenditure on curative and rehabilitative day care

Public expenditure on long-term nursing day care

Private expenditure on day care

Private expenditure on curative and rehabilitative day care

Private expenditure on long-term nursing day care

Expenditure on out-patient care

Total expenditure on out-patient care

Total expenditure on physician services

Total expenditure on dental services

All other total expenditure on out-patient care

Public expenditure on out-patient care

Public expenditure on physician services

Public expenditure on dental services

All other public expenditure on out-patient care

Private expenditure on out-patient care

Expenditure on home care

Total expenditure on home health care

Total expenditure on curative and rehabilitative home care

Total expenditure on long-term nursing home care

Public expenditure on home health care

Public expenditure on curative and rehabilitative home care

Public expenditure on long-term nursing home care

Private expenditure on home health care

Private expenditure on curative and rehabilitative home care

Private expenditure on long-term nursing home care

Expenditure on ancillary services

Total expenditure on ancillary services

Total expenditure on clinical laboratory

Total expenditure on diagnostic imaging

Total expenditure on patient transport and emergency rescue

All other total miscellaneous ancillary services
Public expenditure on ancillary services
Public expenditure on clinical laboratory
Public expenditure on diagnostic imaging
Public expenditure on patient transport and emergency rescue
All other public miscellaneous ancillary services
Private expenditure on ancillary services

Medical goods dispensed to out-patients

Total expenditure on medical goods
Total expenditure on medical goods
Public expenditure on medical goods
Private expenditure on medical goods

Pharmaceuticals & other medical non-durables
Total expenditure on pharmaceuticals and other medical non-durables
Total expenditure on prescription medicines
Total expenditure on over-the-counter medicines
Other medical non-durables
Public expenditure on pharmaceuticals and other medic.non-durables
Private expenditure on pharmaceuticals and other medical non-durables

Therapeutic appliances & other medical durables
Total expenditure on therapeutic appliances and other medical durables
Public expenditure on therapeutic appliances and other medical durables
Private expenditure on therapeutic appliances and other medical durables

Current health expenditure by provider
Total expenditure on hospitals' services
Public expenditure on hospitals' services
Private expenditure on hospitals' services
Total expenditure on services of nursing and residential care facilities
Public expenditure on services of nursing and residential care facilities
Private expenditure on services of nursing and residential care facilities
Total expenditure on services of ambulatory health care providers
Public expenditure on services of ambulatory

health care providers
Private expenditure on services of ambulatory health care providers
Total expenditure for retail sale and other providers of medical goods
Public expenditure for retail sale and other providers of medical goods
Private expenditure for retail sale and other providers of medical goods
Total expenditure on services of public health organisations
Public expenditure on services of public health organisations
Private expenditure on services of public health organisations
Total expenditure on services of health care administration
Public expenditure on services of health care administration
Private expenditure on services of health care administration
Total expenditure on health services of other industries
Public expenditure on health services of other industries
Private expenditure on health services of other industries

Expenditure by age and gender
Women 65+ / Women 0-64
Women 75+ / Women 0-64
Women 65-74 / Women 0-64
Men 65+ / Men 0-64
Men 75+ / Men 0-64
Men 65-74 / Men 0-64
Population 65+ / Population 0-64
Population 75+ / Population 0-64
Population 65-74 / Population 0-64
Expenditure: Population (total)
Expenditure: population aged 0-64 years
Expenditure: population aged 65 and over
Expenditure: population aged 65-74 years
Expenditure: population aged 75 and over

Price index
Total expenditure on health
Total expenditure on pharmaceuticals and other medical non-durables

Public expenditure on health
Private consumption on health

PART 5 - HEALTH CARE FINANCING

Health expenditure by sources of funds

General government, excluding social security
Social security schemes
Out-of-pocket payments (households)
Private insurance
Private insurance (other than social insurance)
Private social insurance
All other private funds (including rest of the world)

PART 6 - SOCIAL PROTECTION

Social expenditure

Total social expenditure
Old age
Survivors
Incapacity-related benefits
Health
Family
Active labour market programmes
Unemployment
Housing
Other social policy areas

Health care coverage

Total health care
In-patient acute care
Out-patient medical care
Pharmaceutical goods

PART 7 - PHARMACEUTICAL MARKET

Pharmaceutical industry activity

Pharmaceutical production
Pharmaceutical value added
Pharmaceutical industry gross capital formation
Pharmaceutical industry exports (manu facturing)
Pharmaceutical industry imports (manu facturing)
Expenditure on pharmaceutical industry R&D

Pharmaceutical industry employees
Pharmaceutical labour compensation

Pharmaceutical consumption

Alimentary Tract and Metabolism
Antacids
Drugs for peptic ulcer & gastro-oesophageal reflux disease
Drugs used in diabetes
Blood and Blood Forming Organs
Cardiovascular System
Cardiac glycosides
Antiarrhythmics, Class I and III
Antihypertensives
Diuretics
Beta blocking agents
Calcium channel blockers
Agents acting on the Renin-Angiotensin system
Cholesterol and triglyceride reducers
Sex hormones and modulators of the genital system
Antiinfectives for Systemic Use
Antibacterials for systemic use
Musculo-Skeletal System
Antiinflammatory & antirheumatic products non-steroids
Nervous System
Analgesics
Anxiolytics
Hypnotics and sedatives
Antidepressants
Respiratory System
Drugs for obstructive airway disease

Pharmaceutical sales

Total pharmaceutical sales
A-Alimentary tract and metabolism
B-Blood and blood forming organs
C-Cardiovascular system
D-Dermatologicals
G-Genitourinary and sex hormones
H-Systemic hormonal preparations, excluding sex hormones & insulins
J- Antiinfectives for systemic use
L-Antineoplastic and immunomodulating agents
M-Musculo-skeletal system
N-Nervous system

P-Antiparasitic products, insecticides and repellents
R-Respiratory system
S-Sensory organs
V-Various
Products not elsewhere classified

PART 8 - NON-MEDICAL DETERMINANTS OF HEALTH

Life styles and behaviour

Food consumption
Total calories intake
Total protein intake
Butter consumption
Sugar consumption
Fruits and vegetables

Alcohol consumption
Alcohol consumption

Tobacco consumption
Tobacco consumption

Body weight and composition
Overweight population
Obese population
Overweight or obese population

Environment: air quality
Total sulphur oxide emissions
Total nitrogen oxide emissions
Total carbon monoxide emissions

PART 9 - DEMOGRAPHIC REFERENCES

General demographics
Total population
Female population
Male population
Fertility
Birth
Death
Age dependency ratio

Population age structure
Total population

Population: 0 to 14 years old
Population: 0 to 19 years old
Population: 15 years old and over
Population: 15 to 49 years old
Population: 15 to 64 years old
Population: 20 to 64 years old
Population: 65 years old and over
Population: 65 to 69 years old
Population: 70 to 74 years old
Population: 75 to 79 years old
Population: 80 years old and over

Labour force
Labour force
Total employment
Total civilian employment
Wage and salaried employment
Part-time employment
Total unemployment

Educational level
Attainment ISCED 0/1/2
Attainment ISCED 3/4
Attainment ISCED 5B
Attainment ISCED 5A/6
School expectancy
Total public and private expenditure for educational institutions

PART 10 - ECONOMIC REFERENCES

Macro-economic references
Gross domestic product
Government final consumption expenditure
Final consumption expenditure of households
Gross fixed capital formation
General government total outlays
Public revenue
Compensation of employees
Average earnings of production worker
Government budget outlays for total R&D

Monetary conversion rates
GDP purchasing power parity, US$
Pharmacy purchasing power parity, US$
US$ exchange rate

BIBLIOGRAPHY

Most recent OECD publications in the Health field

HEALTH AT A GLANCE : OECD Indicators 2003 (2003)

SOCIETY AT A GLANCE (2002)
OECD Social indicators, Edition 2002

MEASURING UP: IMPROVING HEALTH SYSTEMS PERFORMANCE IN OECD COUNTRIES (2002)

OECD SOCIAL EXPENDITURE DATABASE, 1980-1998 (2001)
Available in English and French on CD-ROM

REFORMS FOR AN AGEING SOCIETY (2000)

A SYSTEM OF HEALTH ACCOUNTS (2000)

Health Working Papers

A new series designed to make available to a wider readership health studies prepared for use within the OECD. Available for free download under www.oecd.org/els/health/workingpapers.

Latest issues include:

Health-Care Systems: Lessons from the Reform Experience (OECD Health Working Papers No.9) December 2003

Private Health Insurance in Australia: A Case Study (OECD Health Working Papers No.8) October 2003

Explaining Waiting Times Variations for Elective Surgery across OECD Countries (OECD Health Working Paper No.7) October 2003

Tackling Excessive Waiting Times for Elective Surgery: A Comparison of Policies in Twelve OECD Countries (OECD Health Working Paper No.6) July 2003

Stroke Care in OECD Countries: A Comparison of Treatment, Costs and Outcomes in 17 Countries (OECD Health Working Papers NO.5) June 2003

Survey of Pharmacoeconomic Assessment Activity in Eleven Countries (OECD Health Working Paper NO.4) May 2003

OECD Study of Cross-National Differences in the Treatment, Costs and Outcomes of Ischaemic Heart Disease (OECD Health Working Paper NO.3) April 2003

Investment in Population Health in Five OECD Countries (OECD Health Working Paper N°2) April 2003

Pharmaceutical Use and Expenditure for Cardiovascular Disease and Stroke: a Study of 12 OECD Countries (OECD Health Working Papers No.1) February 2003

Health-related Social Policy Occasional Papers

Available for free download under
http://www.oecd.org/findDocument/0,2350,en_2649_33929_1_119684_1_2_1,00.html.

Most recent releases are:

For a full list of OECD publications, consult the OECD Online Bookshop at:
www.oecd.org/bookshop
or write for a free printed catalogue to the following address:
OECD Publications Service
2, rue André-Pascal, 75775 PARIS CEDEX 16

ECO-SANTÉ OCDE 2004

ANALYSE COMPARATIVE DE 30 PAYS

Guide de l'utilisateur

ECO-SANTÉ OCDE 2004 a été réalisé conjointement par le Secrétariat de l'OCDE et l'IRDES (Institut de Recherche et d'Etude en Economie de la Santé).

L'équipe d'*Eco-Santé OCDE 2004* se compose de Gaëlle Balestat, Marie-Clémence Canaud, Manfred Huber, Gaetan Lafortune, David Morgan et Eva Orosz. L'équipe de l'IRDES se compose de Catherine Banchereau, Martine Broïdo, Jacques Harrouin, Christophe Lainé, Florence Naudin et Thierry Rochereau.

Français

Pour toute question concernant les données et les sources et méthodes, adressez-vous à :	**Pour tout support technique,** adressez-vous à :
L'Unité des Politiques de Santé à l'OCDE 2, rue André Pascal F-75775 Paris Cedex 16 (France) Fax : (33) 1 44 30 63 61 E-mail : health.contact@oecd.org	**IRDES** 10, rue Vauvenargues F-75018 Paris (France) Fax : (33) 1 53 93 43 50 (à l'attention de l'équipe Eco-Santé) E-mail : ecosante@irdes.fr Web : www.irdes.fr

Questions Fréquemment Posées

Les sites Internet de l'OCDE et de l'IRDES s'efforceront de diffuser rapidement des réponses aux questions types qui se poseront en 2004, ainsi que des mises à jour des données, des informations complémentaires sur les variables, des exemples de tableaux et des informations sur la date de sortie prévue d'*Eco-Santé OCDE 2005*

- Pour les problèmes techniques, consultez : www.irdes.fr/ecosante/faq.htm
- Pour les informations et mises à jour des données : www.oecd.org/health/healthdata/ et cliquez sur le bouton **[Frequently Asked Questions]** depuis la page *Eco-Santé OCDE*.

Consultez les sites **Internet** de l'OCDE et de l'IRDES :

- www.oecd.org/health/healthdata/
- www.irdes.fr/ecosante/index.htm

Le logiciel *Eco-Santé OCDE* se compose :

- d'un CD-ROM contenant le programme et les fichiers ;
- de ce guide d'utilisation.

AVANT-PROPOS

Après plus de quinze ans de collecte de séries statistiques, l'OCDE en est à sa treizième édition de cette base de données électronique sur les systèmes de santé.

L'édition 2004 comprend de nouvelles données dans un logiciel amélioré. Les définitions standards des variables et la documentation des sources et méthodes par pays s'y rattachant ont été profondément révisées et enrichies. Grâce aux apports des fournisseurs originaux des données, ces fichiers constituent un outil très riche qui éclaire et aide à comprendre l'évolution ou le niveau des séries. Enfin, pour la version sous environnement Windows 98/2000/NT/Me/XP, diverses fonctionnalités d'*Eco-Santé OCDE* ont été revues et des aménagements ont été apportés à ce logiciel convivial qui a fait ses preuves et bénéficie de l'estime de milliers d'utilisateurs.

Le soutien financier des Centers for Medicare and Medicaid Services (CMS, ex-HCFA) aux Etats-Unis a considérablement facilité la mise au point du logiciel comme du cadre analytique qui sous-tend l'apport de l'OCDE à la mise sur pied d'un système comptable en santé. Le logiciel doit aussi beaucoup à des centaines de statisticiens dans les 30 pays Membres, qui ont produit la grande masse de chiffres et d'informations qualitatives sur lesquels il s'appuie.

Français

INTRODUCTION

Eco-Santé OCDE 2004 présente de façon interactive et systématique des données sur un grand nombre d'aspects des systèmes de santé des 30 pays Membres de l'OCDE, dans leur contexte démographique, économique et social en général.

La version 2004 du logiciel *Eco-Santé OCDE* sous Windows est d'une utilisation très conviviale et rapide. Elle permet aux utilisateurs d'un micro-ordinateur d'interroger les fichiers Santé de l'OCDE et de les analyser à partir de tableaux, graphiques ou représentations cartographiques. *Eco-Santé OCDE* offre également des options d'exportation des données pour utilisation avec d'autres logiciels. L'utilisateur sélectionne les variables, les pays et les années de son choix. Les données regroupent quelque 1200 séries et couvrent la période 1960-2002 avec des séries longues commençant en 1960. La plupart des données couvrent les années 1980 et 1990, de nombreuses séries vont jusqu'en 2001 ou 2002, et des estimations du Secrétariat de l'OCDE pour l'année 2003 sont publiées.

Eco-Santé OCDE 2004 est conçu en version quadrilingue (français/anglais/allemand/espagnol) sous Windows 98/2000/NT/Me/XP. Il a été créé conjointement par l'OCDE et le IRDES. Il est le fruit de l'expérience de ces deux organismes dans des domaines d'études complémentaires :

- La publication et la mise à jour d'indicateurs statistiques sur la santé et ses politiques économiques dans les 30 pays Membres de l'OCDE ;

- Le développement d'un logiciel qui comprend des données macro-économiques décrivant le fonctionnement d'un système de santé.

Ce guide a pour objet de fournir à l'utilisateur du logiciel des informations sur le contenu de ces bases de données, sur les fonctions d'analyse qu'il offre, ainsi que sur sa mise en oeuvre pratique.

NOUVEAUTÉS DE LA VERSION 2004 D'*ECO-SANTÉ OCDE*

La version 2004 d'*Eco-Santé OCDE* contient un certain nombre d'améliorations et de nouveautés :

- Nouvelle procédure d'installation ;

- Application complètement relookée pour respecter les styles XP ;

- Ajout d'un système de recherche dans les *Sources et Méthodes* par mots clef et par texte intégral, et d'un système de navigation dans la structure avec index ;

- Nouvelles fonctions d'impression et d'export pour les *Définitions, Sources et Méthodes* ;

- Logiciel et liste des variables disponibles en russe ;

- Options de changement de langues optimisées (un click pour faire passer tous les modules dans une même langue) ;

- Résultats préliminaires du Projet Santé de l'OCDE inclus dans l'hypertexte.

> Les modifications ou ajouts de dernière minute apportés à *Eco-Santé OCDE 2004* sont présentés dans le fichier **LisezMoi.txt**. Ce fichier pourra être consulté à la fin de la procédure d'installation. Pour le lire ultérieurement, il vous suffit de cliquer sur l'icône LisezMoi dans le dossier *Eco-Santé OCDE 2004*.

Français

Caractéristiques minimales de l'équipement nécessaire et configuration du système

Pour utiliser ce logiciel, il vous faut disposer :

- de Windows 98/2000/NT/Me/XP ;
- de 64 Mo de RAM ;
- de 70 Mo d'espace disponible sur votre disque dur ;
- d'un lecteur de CD-ROM (le CD-ROM n'est utile que pendant la phase d'installation du logiciel) ;
- Carte graphique: 16 bits 800X600.

Si vous disposez d'une version antérieure d'*Eco-Santé OCDE*, il est conseillé de la supprimer afin de ne pas encombrer inutilement le disque dur de votre ordinateur. Pour cela vous devez sélectionner l'icône Ajout/Suppression de programmes dans le Panneau de configuration. Veuillez noter que votre librairie personnelle de tableaux sauvegardés ne peut être transférée d'une version d'*Eco-Santé OCDE* à l'autre.

Installation d'*Eco-Santé OCDE 2004*

Pour amorcer la procédure d'installation, lancez Windows et insérez le CD-ROM dans le lecteur. Les spécificités de l'installation d'*Eco-Santé OCDE* **version réseau** sont explicitées dans un encadré à l'attention de l'administrateur du réseau.

Vous devez fermer toutes les applications et désactiver l'anti-virus de votre PC avant de procéder à l'installation du logiciel. Veuillez également vérifier que vous possédez les droits d'installation d'un logiciel sur votre PC, en consultant votre administrateur réseau, ou l'administrateur de votre PC.

Le CD-ROM n'est utile que pendant la phase d'installation du logiciel.

- Cliquez sur le bouton **[Démarrer]** et sélectionnez **[Exécuter]**.
- Sur la ligne **[Ouvrir]** tapez «d:\install» lorsque votre lecteur de CD-ROM est le lecteur d ;
- Confirmez votre choix par **[OK]**.

Lorsque votre lecteur de CD-ROM est configuré en «AutoBoot», l'installation d'*Eco-Santé OCDE* se lance automatiquement dès l'introduction du CD-ROM dans le lecteur.

L'installation se déroule en cinq étapes :

- Sélectionnez la langue désirée pour l'installation : allemand, anglais, espagnol, français ;
- Vous devez accepter le contrat de licence du logiciel ;
- Introduisez les informations concernant l'utilisateur ainsi que le **numéro de série** du CD-ROM, que vous trouverez sur **la couverture intérieure de ce Guide utilisateur**. Si ce numéro est correct, la procédure d'installation se poursuit. Dans le cas contraire, un message d'erreur s'affiche et vous devez

ressaisir le numéro de série ;

- Choisissez le dossier d'installation du logiciel. Une vérification de l'espace disponible s'effectue. Lorsqu'il n'y a pas assez de place sur le disque, l'utilisateur doit libérer de la place ou changer le disque de destination ;
- La dernière fenêtre demande une confirmation des choix effectués avant de lancer la copie des composants du logiciel.

A la fin de la procédure d'installation un dossier/groupe est créé, contenant les icônes nécessaires à l'utilisation d'*Eco-Santé OCDE 2004*.

Une fenêtre apparaît alors, vous donnant les contacts utiles en cas de questions sur le logiciel, ainsi que les adresses des sites Internet de l'OCDE et de l'IRDES.

NB : L'utilisateur peut être amené à relancer son ordinateur suite au processus d'installation, ce qui lui sera notifié par le programme si tel est le cas.

Spécificités de l'installation d'*Eco-Santé OCDE* en réseau

Pour installer la version réseau, l'administrateur du réseau doit commencer par installer la partie «serveur» du logiciel sur un lecteur réseau accessible à tous les utilisateurs potentiels. Cette procédure est identique à l'installation standard (voir ci-dessus). Puis, l'administrateur doit installer la partie «client» sur chaque poste. Pour cela il doit lancer le programme Install.exe se trouvant dans le sous répertoire USER. Par exemple si vous avez installé le logiciel sur le disque E:\APPLI\ECOSANTE2004, la commande pour installer les postes sera : E:\APPLI\ECOSANTE2004\USER\INSTALL.EXE

Le programme d'installation de la partie «client» crée automatique un répertoire c:\ecowin2004. Si vous désirez déplacer le répertoire « local » de l'utilisateur vous devez aussi modifier le paramètre **LocalPath** dans le fichier **Ecowin.ini** qui se trouve dans le répertoire windows.

Les travaux sauvegardés par les utilisateurs se placent par défaut dans leur répertoire «local». Grâce à ce répertoire «local», chaque utilisateur peut disposer de ses propres groupes de pays et tableaux sauvegardés. La partie client occupe moins de 1 méga octet sur le disque de l'utilisateur.

Démarrer *Eco-Santé OCDE 2004*

Choisissez **[Démarrer - Programmes - Eco-Santé OCDE 2004]** et positionnez-vous sur **[Eco-Santé]**.

Pour permettre un bon fonctionnement du logiciel, il est important que le disque dur dispose d'au moins 5 Mo de place disponible après l'installation, afin de stocker les fichiers de travail et de sauvegarde.

Une fois le logiciel lancé, vous pouvez essayer les différentes options en vous laissant guider par des fenêtres successives et en vous référant aux zones d'information des fenêtres.

Des Info-bulles - voir plus bas - sont automatiquement activées lors de la première utilisation du logiciel. Il est cependant conseillé de lire ce guide pour en savoir plus avant l'utilisation pratique du logiciel.

Désinstallation du programme

Pour désinstaller le logiciel, quittez *Eco-Santé*. Cliquez sur le bouton **[Démarrer]**, et choisir «Paramètres». Dans Panneau de configuration, sélectionnez l'icône **[Ajout/Suppression]** de programmes. Choisissez **[Eco-Santé OCDE 2004]** dans la liste et cliquez sur **[Ajouter/Supprimer]**. Cliquer sur **[OK]** pour confirmer la suppression de l'application.

Ce programme supprime tous les fichiers d'*Eco-Santé OCDE 2004*. La désinstallation du programme ne nécessite pas l'utilisation du CD-ROM.

Mise à jour des données par le biais d'Internet

Certaines erreurs peuvent se glisser dans des séries statistiques, des mises à jour ou des données supplémentaires peuvent devenir disponibles après la publication d'*Eco-Santé OCDE*. Il est hautement souhaitable d'intégrer ces nouvelles valeurs dans votre logiciel au moyen de l'un ou l'autre des deux sites d'Internet cités ci-après.

Au niveau d'Internet :

- Connectez-vous sur un des sites suivants, en cliquant sur les logos de l'OCDE ou de l'IRDES à partir du menu principal :

  ⇨ le site de l'OCDE : www.oecd.org/health/healthdata/ ;

  ⇨ le site de l'IRDES : www.irdes.fr/ecosante/index.htm ;

- Cliquez sur le bouton **[Updates]** depuis le site de l'OCDE et sur **[Mise à jour des données]** depuis le site de l'IRDES ;

- Double-cliquez sur **[Chargement]** (**[Download]**) et indiquez le répertoire de votre micro-ordinateur dans lequel copier les fichiers téléchargés.

Sous Windows :

- Une fois le fichier téléchargé, double-cliquez sur l'icône (ou le mot) pour démarrer l'installation ;
- Le fichier téléchargé est en fait un fichier compressé auto-extractible (.EXE) contenant 2 fichiers :

  ⇨ la mise à jour de la base de données proprement dite ;

  ⇨ un fichier LisezMoi.TXT qui explique ces mises à jour.

- Entrez le nom du répertoire dans lequel vous avez installé votre base de données *Eco-Santé OCDE 2004* (par exemple c:\software\ecowin2004), et validez votre choix ;

- La procédure de mise à jour va se lancer , avec le titre de la base et sa version (par exemple *Eco-Santé OCDE 2004* . 2ème édition.) : cliquez sur « Start update » pour lancer la mise à jour.

- Si la mise à jour ne se lance pas, veuillez vérifier le nom du répertoire dans lequel la base est installée et le ressaisir.

Dans la fenêtre principale d'*Eco-Santé OCDE 2004*:

Une fois la mise à jour effectuée, la date et le nom de la version sous le titre «*ECO-SANTÉ OCDE 2004*» sont modifiés.

CHAPITRE DEUX : INTERROGATION DE LA BASE DE DONNEES

Menu principal d'*Eco-Santé OCDE 2004*

Les différentes fonctions du logiciel sont sélectionnées par l'intermédiaire de boutons. Un simple clic sur l'un de ces boutons permet d'effectuer l'action inhérente à la fonctionnalité désirée ou d'arriver à un écran permettant la réalisation de cette fonction après sélection de différents paramètres.

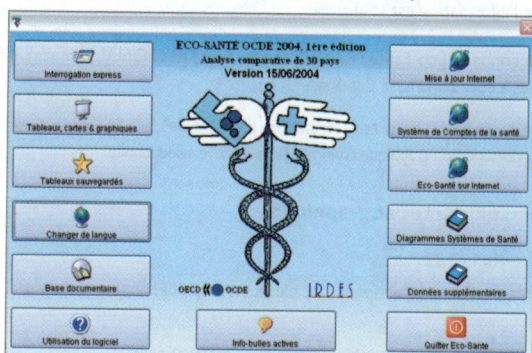

[Interrogation express] permet de sélectionner une variable pour en obtenir les valeurs dans un pays ou dans l'ensemble des pays, pour une, deux ou toutes les années disponibles, et de calculer des taux de croissance sur la période correspondante. Cette fonction permet la construction de cartes, ainsi que l'impression ou l'exportation du tableau réalisé.	**[Sources et méthodes]** donne accès au sommaire de l'aide à l'utilisation des variables, c'est à dire aux définitions, et sources et méthodes attachées. **[Utilisation du logiciel]** donne accès au sommaire de l'aide sur le logiciel.
[Tableaux, cartes & graphiques] permet de sélectionner une ou plusieurs variables pour en obtenir les valeurs dans un ou plusieurs pays, pour une ou plusieurs années, et de calculer des taux de croissance annuels moyens sur la période correspondante. Cette fonction conduit aussi à la construction de cartes et de graphiques.	**[Info-bulles]** active ou désactive la visualisation de l'information sur les boutons et objets du logiciel
[Tableaux sauvegardés] permet de récupérer un tableau préalablement sauvegardé par vos soins, ou prédéfini par l'Unité des Politiques de Santé. Vous pouvez ainsi sauvegarder votre propre librairie de tableaux.	**Accès direct à Internet :** les boutons portant ce logo donnent accès à des sites Internet OCDE liés à la santé, ainsi qu'à la page de téléchargement de la mise à jour Internet.
[Changement de langue] permet de choisir une langue de travail pour le logiciel (allemand, anglais, espagnol ou français) ainsi que pour l'aide (anglais ou français).	**[Quitter Eco-Santé]** termine la session.

Aides

Aide à l'utilisation des variables : Sources et Méthodes

Les Sources et Méthodes attachées aux variables sont accessibles de manière contextuelle ou via un index général.

Pour obtenir cette assistance contextuelle, cliquez avec le bouton droit de la souris sur l'élément pour lequel vous désirez la définition de référence, la source et/ou l'écart par rapport à la définition de référence. Dans *Eco-Santé OCDE 2004*, cette aide est accessible à partir des listes des chapitres et variables.

Pour accéder à l'index général de l'aide à l'utilisation des variables (Sources & Méthodes), cliquez sur le bouton **[Sources]** lorsqu'il est disponible. Sélectionnez le chapitre, puis la variable pour laquelle l'information est souhaitée.

Deux autres bases de données, Eco-Santé FRANCE et Eco-Santé REGIONAL (France), diffusées par l'IRDES, peuvent être installées à côté de la base *Eco-Santé OCDE*.

Lorsque au moins deux de ces bases sont présentes, une liste déroulante en face de «base active» permet la sélection de l'une d'entre elles. La représentation graphique confirme la base active sélectionnée.

Création de tableaux, cartes et graphiques

Sélection des variables

Le choix d'une variable consiste à sélectionner les paramètres qui définissent cette variable sur trois onglets. Il faut ainsi choisir :

- le **chapitre**, auquel se rattache la variable désirée *(ex. Emploi en santé)* ;

- la **variable**, parmi celles qui sont associées au chapitre choisi *(ex. Pharmaciens en activité)* ;

- l'**unité**, parmi celles associées aux deux choix précédents *(ex. taux pour 1000 habitants)*.

Pour accéder à la liste des variables, cliquez sur le bouton **[Ajouter]** de l'onglet **«Variables»** ou dans la zone vide de l'onglet.

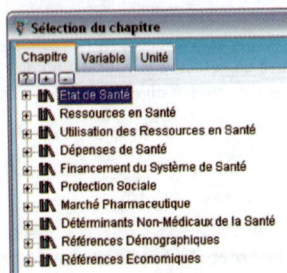

⇨ Les intitulés des chapitres, variables et unités figurent sur l'écran de façon abrégée, mais suffisamment explicite.

⇨ Leur enchaînement logique permet de choisir sans difficulté la séquence qui mène à la variable recherchée. Toutefois, une liste des variables est consultable dans le Chapitre 3 de ce guide.

Sur l'onglet **«chapitre»**, trois boutons sont disponibles :

Un clic sur le bouton **[+]** fait apparaître, pour l'ensemble des chapitres d'un niveau, le détail du niveau inférieur (le clic sur le bouton **[+]** peut être opéré pour les différents niveaux : pour obtenir tous les chapitres «parents» contenus dans les chapitres «grands-parents», puis tous les chapitres «enfants» contenus dans les chapitres «parents»). Inversement, un clic sur le bouton **[-]** de cet onglet réduit le détail proposé au niveau inférieur. Un clic sur **[?]** vous donne accés à l'aide sur le logiciel.

Multisélection

Il existe un autre moyen de sélection des variables communes à plusieurs chapitres. Mais cette nouvelle procédure nécessite toutefois de connaître préalablement le contenu des chapitres en question.

Pour cela, cliquer dans la case **[Multisélection]**.

Des cases apparaissent devant le nom des chapitres : cliquez dans chacune des cases correspondant aux chapitres contenant les variables que vous recherchez.

Le choix des chapitres arrêté, cliquez sur la flèche **[Suivant]**. Vous vous trouvez alors sur un écran de choix de variables. Cet écran ne vous présente plus que les variables communes aux chapitres précédemment sélectionnés. La suite (choix de la ou des variables, choix de l'unité ou des unités) est la même que précédemment.

Sélection des pays

Pour accéder à la sélection des pays, cliquez sur l'onglet **«Pays»**.

La liste des pays de l'OCDE se trouve en haut de la fenêtre à gauche ; les groupes de pays se situent en bas de cette fenêtre ; à droite se trouve la fenêtre dans laquelle s'afficheront les pays ou groupes de pays sélectionnés.

Sélection d'un pays (ou de quelques pays)

Pour sélectionner un pays :

- soit cliquez deux fois sur le pays désiré,
- soit cliquez une fois sur ce pays, puis cliquez sur le bouton **[+]**.

Pour sélectionner tous les pays, cliquez sur le bouton **[++]**. Pour désactiver la sélection d'un ou de plusieurs pays, cliquez respectivement sur **[-]** ou **[- -]**

Tous les pays passent alors dans la fenêtre de droite.

Diagrammes sur les Systèmes de Santé

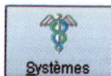

Cette aide à la compréhension des systèmes de santé est accessible de manière contextuelle ou via un index général. Elle comprend, pour la plupart des pays de l'OCDE, des diagrammes descriptifs des acteurs intervenants sur le «marché» des soins de santé et de leurs interrelations.

Dans certains cas, deux ou plusieurs graphiques sont présentés pour un pays, afin d'illustrer l'évolution des réformes de santé dans ce pays pendant la dernière décennie ou plus. L'assistance contextuelle est accessible en cliquant avec le bouton droit de la souris sur le pays pour lequel vous désirez obtenir l'aide.

Pour accéder à l'index général des systèmes, cliquez sur le bouton **[Systèmes]**. Sélectionnez le pays pour lequel l'information est souhaitée.

Sélection des années et périodes

Pour calculer des taux de croissance qui requièrent la sélection préalable d'années et de périodes, cliquez sur l'onglet **«Années et périodes»**.

La colonne de gauche **«Années disponibles»** affiche l'ensemble des années pour lesquelles il y a des chiffres. Toutes les années n'ayant pas des chiffres pour chaque variable et l'ensemble des pays, un clic sur le bouton **[Disponibilité]** en bas à droite dans la fenêtre permet de visualiser ce qu'il en est.

Boutons bleus = années pour lesquelles des chiffres sont disponibles
Boutons verts = années sélectionnées

Visualisation du tableau

Préalablement à la visualisation d'un tableau, la mise en garde suivante apparaît, concernant les précautions à prendre lors de comparaisons de variables entre différents pays.

Cliquez sur **[OK]** pour visualiser les données.

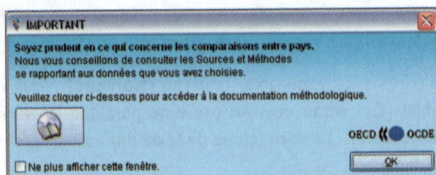

Barre d'outils des tableaux

La barre d'outils comprend des icônes dont la signification est :

	Réduit / augmente la taille de la barre d'outils.
	Réduit /augmente la taille de la feuille active.
	Règle la largeur de toutes les colonnes de façon automatique (la largeur de chaque colonne est alors déterminée par son contenu).
	Permet de fixer la même largeur pour toutes les colonnes du tableau en prenant pour référence la colonne active.
	Active/désactive le quadrillage.
	Affiche/ferme la fenêtre des légendes.
	Trie les éléments du tableau par ordre croissant ou décroissant à partir des données contenues dans la colonne active.
	Permet de supprimer une colonne du tableau, dont il faut préciser la position (par défaut, la position indiquée est celle de la colonne active).
	Permet de calculer un indice comparatif.
	Permet d'ajouter une colonne donnant le rang.
	Permet de faire la moyenne arithmétique des valeurs de la colonne active (le résultat apparaît sur la dernière ligne).

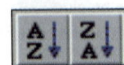

Σ	Permet de faire la somme des valeurs de la colonne active (le résultat apparaît sur la dernière ligne).
	Conduit à l'écran de paramétrage de l'impression du tableau.
	Conduit à l'écran d'exportation des tableaux.
	Permet de copier la zone active dans le presse-papiers et de coller son contenu dans une autre application Windows (option **[Coller]** du menu édition ou raccourci **[CTRL+V]**).
	Donne accès au module de construction des graphiques.
	Permet de construire une carte à partir de la colonne sélectionnée, lorsque les lignes du tableau sont des pays.
	Donne accès à l'aide à l'utilisation du logiciel.
	Donne accès à l'aide à l'utilisation des variables (Sources et Méthodes).
	Permet de quitter l'écran de visualisation du tableau.

Pour modifier l'intitulé des colonnes, double-cliquez sur celles-ci. Pour modifier le titre du tableau, double-cliquez dans la cellule vide en haut à gauche du tableau.

Ces fonctionnalités de la barre d'outils sont directement accessibles en utilisant le clic droit sur le titre d'une colonne, depuis un tableau. Un clic droit sur le titre d'un indicateur (quand les variables sont en ligne et les années ou pays en colonne) mène directement à la définition, source et méthode de l'indicateur choisi.

Exportation du tableau

Le paramétrage de l'exportation est accessible à partir de la barre d'outils dans l'écran **«Visualisation»**.

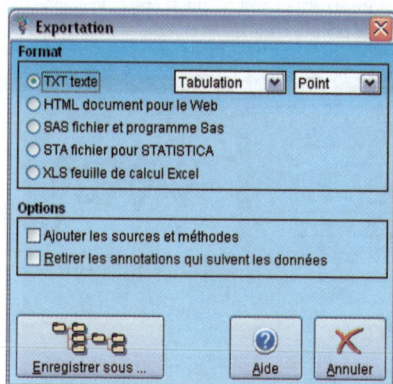

Cinq modes d'exportation sont proposés :

● **Texte .TXT**

Cette option permet d'obtenir un fichier texte facilement utilisable, avec choix de séparateur de colonnes : tabulation, espace, virgule, point-virgule ; et de séparateur de décimales : point ou virgule.

● **Système SAS**

Le système SAS requiert deux fichiers : celui contenant les données (extension «DAT») et celui qui inclut le descriptif des variables et le découpage du fichier de données (extension «SAS»). Pour importer ce fichier sous SAS, il faut exécuter le programme. Celui-ci génère, à partir du fichier de données, un fichier dans le répertoire temporaire de SAS (Work), dont le résultat se consulte dans l'environnement SAS (Pour de plus amples informations sur SAS : www.sas.com/).

Cliquez sur le bouton **[Enregistrer sous]** pour choisir le chemin de la sauvegarde. Une nouvelle fenêtre apparaît alors indiquant par défaut le répertoire dans lequel sauvegarder vos fichiers. Suivant les procédures propres à Windows, vous pouvez naviguer dans les différents répertoires pour choisir le répertoire où placer vos fichiers. Donnez un nom à votre fichier sur la ligne Fichier de cette fenêtre. Par défaut, l'extension est celle correspondant au format d'exportation que vous avez choisi. Cliquez sur le bouton **[Enregistrer]**. Un message «Fichier sauvegardé» avertit du bon déroulement de l'exportation du fichier. Cliquez sur le bouton **[Annuler]** pour revenir à la fenêtre **«Exportation»**.

● **STA fichier pour STATISTICA**

Ce format d'exportation permet de créer un fichier ayant l'extension .STA pour le logiciel de statistique Statistica de la société StatSoft (www.statsoft.com/). Le fichier comprend le titre du tableau, les données ainsi que les libellés des variables.

● **HTML**

Ce format permet de créer un tableau que vous pourrez visualiser à l'aide d'un explorateur Internet comme Netscape ou Internet Explorer. Ce type de document a l'avantage de pouvoir être visualisé directement sur l'ensemble des ordinateurs (PC, Macintosh, Station Unix, etc.).

● **Excel .XLS**

Ce format permet de récupérer directement les données sous Excel, version 4.0 et plus, sans avoir à convertir leur format. Les titres du tableau exporté apparaissent dans une cellule de la feuille Excel en haut et à gauche du tableau. (Pour de plus amples informations sur Excel : http://office.microsoft.com/home/default.aspx).

Module graphique

Le module graphique a été amélioré et permet maintenant de créer des graphiques complexes, en sélectionnant les données directement depuis le tableau créé. L'aide en ligne est disponible depuis le bouton «Aide» sur le graphique.

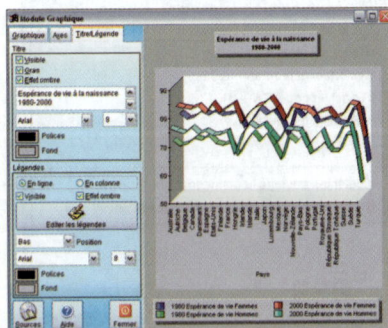

PARTIE I - ETAT DE SANTÉ

Mortalité

Espérance de vie
Femmes à la naissance
Femmes à 40 ans
Femmes à 60 ans
Femmes à 65 ans
Femmes à 80 ans
Hommes à la naissance
Hommes à 40 ans
Hommes à 60 ans
Hommes à 65 ans
Hommes à 80 ans
Femmes et hommes à la naissance

Causes de mortalité
Toutes catégories
Maladies infectieuses et parasitaires
Maladies dues au VIH
Tumeurs malignes
Tumeurs malignes du côlon
Tumeurs malignes du poumon
Tumeurs malignes du sein (femme)
Tumeurs malignes du col de l'utérus
Tumeurs malignes de la prostate
Maladies du sang
Maladies endocriniennes, nutritionnelles et métaboliques
Diabète sucré
Troubles mentaux et du comportement
Maladies du système nerveux
Maladies de l'appareil circulatoire
Cardiopathies ischémiques
Infarctus aigu du myocarde
Maladies cérébrovasculaires
Maladies de l'appareil respiratoire
Grippe et pneumopathie
Bronchite, asthme et emphyséme
Maladies de l'appareil digestif
Hépathite chronique et cirrhose du foie
Maladies de la peau et tissus sous-cutanés

Maladies du système ostéo-musculaire
Maladies du système génito-urinaire
Grossesse, accouchement et puerpéralité
Pathologies périnatales
Malformations congénitales
Symptômes, états mal définis
Causes externes
Accidents de transports
Chutes accidentelles
Lésions auto-infligées
Agressions
Effets indésirables des médicaments
Complications dues à un acte médical

Mortalité infantile et maternelle
Mortalité infantile
Mortalité néonatale
Mortalité périnatale
Mortalité maternelle

Années de vie potentielle perdues
Toutes catégories
Maladies infectieuses et parasitaires
Maladies dues au VIH
Tumeurs malignes
Tumeurs malignes du côlon
Tumeurs malignes du poumon
Tumeurs malignes du sein (femme)
Tumeurs malignes du col de l'utérus
Tumeurs malignes de la prostate
Maladies du sang
Maladies endocriniennes, nutritionnelles et métaboliques
Diabète sucré
Troubles mentaux et du comportement
Maladies du système nerveux
Maladies de l'appareil circulatoire
Cardiopathies ischémiques
Infarctus aigu du myocarde
Maladies cérébrovasculaires
Maladies de l'appareil respiratoire
Grippe et pneumopathie
Bronchite, asthme et emphysème

Français

Maladies de l'appareil digestif
Hépathite chronique et cirrhose du foie
Maladies de la peau et tissus sous-cutanés
Maladies du système ostéo-musculaire
Maladies du système génito-urinaire
Grossesse, accouchement et puerpéralité
Pathologies périnatales
Malformations congénitales
Symptômes, états mal définis
Causes externes
Accidents de transports
Chutes accidentelles
Lésions auto-infligées
Agressions
Effets indésirables des médicaments
Complications dues à un acte médical

Morbidité

Perception de l'état de santé
Santé ≥ bonne, femmes, 15-24
Santé ≥ bonne, femmes, 25-44
Santé ≥ bonne, femmes, 45-64
Santé ≥ bonne, femmes, 65+
Santé ≥ bonne, femmes, tous âges
Santé ≥ bonne, hommes, 15-24
Santé ≥ bonne, hommes, 25-44
Santé ≥ bonne, hommes, 45-64
Santé ≥ bonne, hommes, 65+
Santé ≥ bonne, hommes, tous âges
Santé ≥ bonne, population, 15-24
Santé ≥ bonne, population, 25-44
Santé ≥ bonne, population, 45-64
Santé ≥ bonne, population, 65+
Santé ≥ bonne, population, tous âges

Santé du nourrisson
Hypotrophie à la naissance

Anomalies congénitales
Spina bifida
Transposition des gros vaisseaux
Anomalies de taille des membres
Trisomie 21

Santé buccale
Dents cariées, avulsées, obturées (CAO)

Maladies transmissibles

Syndrôme d'immuno-déficience acquise (SIDA)

Cancer
Tumeurs malignes
Tumeurs malignes du côlon
Tumeurs malignes du poumon
Tumeurs malignes du sein (femmes)
Tumeurs malignes du col de l'utérus
Tumeurs malignes de la prostate

Accidents
Accidents de la circulation

Absentéisme au travail pour cause de maladie
Absentéisme au travail pour cause de maladie, auto-déclaré
Absentéisme au travail pour cause de maladie, indemnisé

PARTIE 2 - RESSOURCES EN SANTÉ

Emploi dans le secteur de la santé

Emploi total en santé
Emploi total dans les hôpitaux
Médecins en activité
Femmes médecins en activité
Médecins généralistes en activité
Spécialistes en activité
Dentistes en activité
Pharmaciens en activité
Infirmiers en activité

Lits d'hôpitaux

Lits, hôpitaux de soins aigus
Lits, maisons médicalisées

Ratio emploi/lits

Personnel, hôpitaux de soins aigus
Infirmiers, hôpitaux de soins aigus

Technologie médicale

Scanners CT
Appareils d'Imagerie par Résonance Magnétique (IRM)
Equipement en radiothérapie
Lithotripteurs
Stations d'hémodialyse
Mammographes

Français

Otite moyenne
Maladies de l'appareil circulatoire
Cardiopathies ischémiques
Infarctus aigu du myocarde
Maladies cérébrovasculaires
Maladies de l'appareil respiratoire
Grippe et pneumopathie
Bronchite, asthme et emphysème
Maladies de l'appareil digestif
Ulcères
Appendicite
Hernie inguinale et fémorale
Hépathite chronique et cirrhose du foie
Cholélithiase
Maladies de la peau et tissus sous-cutanés
Maladies du système ostéo-musculaire
Arthrose
Lésions, disques intervertébraux
Ostéoporose
Maladies du système génito-urinaire
Grossesse, accouchement et puerpéralité
Accouchement unique et spontané
Pathologies périnatales
Malformations congénitales
Symptômes, états mal définis
Causes externes
Fracture du col du fémur
Autres catégories

Procédures chirurgicales

Nombre total d'actes chirurgicaux
Nombre total d'actes chirurgicaux (hospitalisation et ambulatoire)
Nombre total d'actes chirurgicaux avec hospitalisation
Nombre total d'actes de chirurgie ambulatoire

Procédures chirurgicales par CIM-MC
Chirurgie de la cataracte
Amygdalectomie avec ou sans adénoïdectomie
Interventions coronariennes percutanées (angioplastie et stenting)
Stenting coronarien
Pontage coronarien
Catheterisation cardiaque
Pacemakers (stimulateurs cardiaques)
Ligature et stripping des veines
Appendicectomie
Cholécystectomie

Cholécystectomie et laparoscopie
Hernie inguinale et fémorale
Prostatectomie (transurètrale)
Prostatectomie (excluant transurètrale)
Hystérectomie (vaginale)
Césarienne
Prothèse de la hanche
Prothèse du genou
Chirurgie conservatrice du sein
Mastectomie

Greffes et dialyses
Greffe de la moelle osseuse
Greffe du coeur
Greffe du foie
Greffe du poumon
Greffe du rein
Greffons rénaux fonctionnels
Insuffisants rénaux chroniques
Patients dialysés
Patients dialysés à domicile

PARTIE 4 - DÉPENSES DE SANTÉ

Dépenses nationales de santé

Dépenses totales de santé
Dépenses totales de santé
Dépenses totales courantes de santé
Dépenses totales en investissement médical
Dépenses publiques de santé
Dépenses publiques courantes de santé
Dépenses publiques en investissement médical
Dépenses privées de santé
Dépenses privées courantes de santé
Dépenses privées en investissement médical

Dépenses en soins de santé individuels
Dépenses totales en soins de santé individuels
Dépenses publiques en soins de santé individuels
Dépenses privées en soins de santé individuels

Dépenses de santé pour la collectivité
Dépenses totales de santé pour la collectivité
Dépenses publiques de santé pour la collectivité
Dépenses privées de santé pour la collectivité

Prévention et santé publique
Dépenses totales en prévention et santé publique
Dépenses publiques en prévention et santé publique

Dépenses privées en prévention et santé publique

Dépenses d'administration de la santé et assurance maladie
Dépenses totales d'administration et assurances de santé
Dépenses publiques d'administration et assurances de santé
Dépenses privées d'administration et assurances de santé

Dépenses liées à la santé
Dépenses en éducation et formation du personnel de santé
Dépenses totales de R-D en santé
Dépenses publiques de R-D en santé

Dépenses en services médicaux

Dépenses en services médicaux par fonctions
Dépenses totales en services médicaux
Dépenses totales en soins curatifs et réadaptation
Dépenses totales en soins de longue durée
Dépenses totales en services auxiliaires
Dépenses totales en services non classés par fonctions
Dépenses publiques en services médicaux
Dépenses publiques en soins curatifs et réadaptation
Dépenses publiques en soins de longue durée
Dépenses publiques en services auxiliaires
Dépenses publiques en services non classés par fonctions
Dépenses privées en services médicaux
Dépenses privées en soins curatifs et réadaptation
Dépenses privées en soins de longue durée
Dépenses privées en services auxiliaires
Dépenses privées en services non classés par fonctions

Dépenses en soins en milieu hospitalier
Dépenses totales en soins hospitaliers
Dépenses totales en soins curatifs et de réadaptation en hôpital
Dépenses totales en soins de longue durée en milieu hospitalier
Dépenses publiques en soins hospitaliers

Dépenses publiques en soins curatifs et de réadaptation en hôpital
Dépenses publiques en soins de longue durée en milieu hospitalier
Dépenses privées en soins hospitaliers
Dépenses privées en soins curatifs et de réadaptation en hôpital
Dépenses privées en soins de longue durée en milieu hospitalier

Dépenses en soins en hospitalisation de jour
Dépenses totales en hospitalisation de jour
Dépenses totales en soins curatifs et de réadaptation en hospitalisation de jour
Dépenses totales en soins de longue durée en hospitalisation de jour
Dépenses publiques en hospitalisation de jour
Dépenses publiques en soins curatifs et de réadaptation en hospitalisation de jour
Dépenses publiques en soins de longue durée en hospitalisation de jour
Dépenses privées en hospitalisation de jour
Dépenses privées en soins curatifs et de réadaptation en hospitalisation de jour
Dépenses privées en soins de longue durée en hospitalisation de jour

Dépenses en soins ambulatoires
Dépenses totales en soins de patients ambulatoires
Dépenses totales en services de médecins
Dépenses totales en soins dentaires
Dépenses totales en autres soins de patients ambulatoires
Dépenses publiques en soins de patients ambulatoires
Dépenses publiques en services de médecins
Dépenses publiques en soins dentaires
Dépenses publiques en autres soins de patients ambulatoires
Dépenses privées en soins de patients ambulatoires

Dépenses en soins à domicile
Dépenses totales en soins à domicile
Dépenses totales en soins curatifs et de réadaptation à domicile
Dépenses totales en soins de longue durée à domicile
Dépenses publiques en soins à domicile
Dépenses publiques en soins curatifs et de réadaptation à domicile

Français

Dépenses publiques en soins de longue durée à domicile

Dépenses privées en soins à domicile

Dépenses privées en soins curatifs et de réadaptation à domicile

Dépenses privées en soins de longue durée à domicile

Dépenses en services auxiliaires

Dépenses totales en services auxiliaires

Dépenses totales en laboratoires d'analyses médicales

Dépenses totales en imagerie diagnostique

Dépenses totales en transports sanitaires et secours d'urgence

Dépenses totales en autres services auxiliaires

Dépenses publiques en services auxiliaires

Dépenses publiques en laboratoires d'analyse médicales

Dépenses publiques en imagerie diagnostique

Dépenses publiques en transports sanitaires et secours d'urgence

Dépenses publiques en autres services auxiliaires

Dépenses privées en services auxiliaires

Biens médicaux dispensés aux patients ambulatoires

Dépenses totales en biens médicaux

Dépenses totales en biens médicaux

Dépenses publiques en biens médicaux

Dépenses privées en biens médicaux

Produits pharmaceutiques et autres biens médicaux non durables

Dépenses totales en produits pharmaceutiques et autres non-durables

Dépenses totales en médicaments délivrés sur ordonnance

Dépenses totales en médicaments en vente libre

Autres biens médicaux non-durables

Dépenses publiques en produits pharmaceutiques et autres non-durables

Dépenses privées en produits pharmaceutiques et autres non-durables

Appareils thérapeutiques et autres biens médicaux durables

Dépenses totales en appareils thérapeutiques et autres durables

Dépenses publiques en appareils thérapeuti-

ques et autres durables

Dépenses privées en appareils thérapeutiques et autres durables

Dépenses courantes de santé par prestataire de soins

Services fournis par les hôpitaux (dépenses courantes totales)

Services fournis par les hôpitaux (dépenses courantes publiques)

Services fournis par les hôpitaux (dépenses courantes privées)

Maisons médicalisées, soins avec hébergement (dépenses courantes totales)

Maisons médicalisées, soins avec hébergement (dépenses courantes publiques)

Maisons médicalisées, soins avec hébergement (dépenses courantes privées)

Prestataires de soins ambulatoires (dépenses courantes totales)

Prestataires de soins ambulatoires (dépenses courantes publiques)

Prestataires de soins ambulatoires (dépenses courantes privées)

Détaillants et autres distributeurs de biens médicaux (dépenses courantes totales)

Détaillants et autres distributeurs de biens médicaux (dépenses courantes publiques)

Détaillants et autres distributeurs de biens médicaux (dépenses courantes privées)

Services des organisations de santé publique (dépenses courantes totales)

Services des organisations de santé publique (dépenses courantes publiques)

Services des organisations de santé publique (dépenses courantes privées)

Services de l'administration générale de la santé (dépenses courantes totales)

Services de l'administration générale de la santé (dépenses courantes publiques)

Services de l'administration générale de la santé (dépenses courantes privées)

Autres prestataires de services de santé (dépenses courantes totales)

Autres prestataires de services de santé (dépenses courantes publiques)

Autres prestataires de services de santé (dépenses courantes privées)

Français

Système Ostéo-Musculaire
Anti-inflammatoires et anti-rhumatismaux
Système Nerveux
Analgésiques
Anxiolytiques
Hypnotiques et sédatifs
Antidépresseurs
Système Respiratoire
Traitements des maladies des voies aériennes obstruées

Ventes de médicaments
Ventes pharmaceutiques totales
A-Tube digestif et métabolisme
B-Sang et organes hématopoïétiques
C-Système cardio-vasculaire
D-Produits dermatologiques
G-Hormones sexuelles et génito-urinaires
H-Préparations hormonales systémiques
J-Anti-infectieux pour utilisation systémique
L-Anti-cancéreux et agents immunomodulateurs
M-Système ostéo-musculaire
N-Système nerveux
P-Produits antiparasitaires, insecticides et insectifuges
R-Système respiratoire
S-Organes sensoriels
V-Divers
Produits non classés ailleurs

PARTIE 8 - DÉTÉRMINANTS NON-MÉDICAUX DE LA SANTÉ

Mode de vie et environnement

Alimentation
Apport calorique total
Apport protéique total
Consommation de beurre
Consommation de sucre
Consommation de fruits et légumes

Consommation d'alcool
Consommation d'alcool

Consommation de tabac
Consommation de tabac

Masse pondérale
Population souffrant d'excès de poids
Population obèse

Population souffrant d'excès de poids ou obèse

Environnement : qualité de l'air
Emissions d'oxydes de soufre
Emissions d'oxydes d'azote
Emissions de monoxydes de carbone

PARTIE 9 - RÉFÉRENCES DÉMOGRAPHIQUES

Données démographiques générales
Population totale
Population féminine
Population masculine
Fécondité
Natalité
Décès
Dépendance

Population par structure d'âge
Population totale
Population: 0 à 14 ans
Population: 0 à 19 ans
Population: 15 ans et plus
Population: 15 à 49 ans
Population: 15 à 64 ans
Population: 20 à 64 ans
Population: 65 ans et plus
Population: 65 à 69 ans
Population: 70 à 74 ans
Population: 75 à 79 ans
Population: 80 ans et plus

Population active
Population active
Emploi total
Emploi civil total
Emploi salarié
Emploi à mi-temps
Chômage

Niveau d'éducation
Niveau de formation CITE 0/1/2
Niveau de formation CITE 3/4
Niveau de formation CITE 5B
Niveau de formation CITE 5A/6

Espérance de scolarisation
Dépenses totales publiques et privées en institutions éducatives

PARTIE 10 - RÉFÉRENCES ECONOMIQUES

Références macro-économiques

Produit intérieur brut
Consommation finale des administrations publiques
Dépense de consommation finale des ménages
Formation brute de capital fixe
Dépenses totales des administrations publiques
Recettes totales des administrations
Rémunération des salariés
Revenus moyens des ouvriers
Crédits budgétaires de R-D (total)

Taux de conversion monétaire

Parité de pouvoir d'achat du PIB, US$
Parité de pouvoir d'achat pharmacie, US$
Taux de change, US$

Français

BIBLIOGRAPHIE

Publications récentes de l'OCDE dans le domaine de la santé

PANORAMA DE LA SANTÉ : LES INDICATEURS DE L'OCDE 2003 (2003)

PANORAMA DE LA SOCIÉTÉ (2002)
Les indicateurs sociaux de l'OCDE, Édition 2002

ETRE À LA HAUTEUR: MESURER ET AMÉLIORER LA PERFORMANCE DES SYSTÈMES DE SANTÉ DANS LES PAYS DE L'OCDE (2002)

BASE DE DONNÉES DE L'OCDE SUR LES DÉPENSES SOCIALES, 1980-1998 (2001)
Disponible en anglais et français sur CD-ROM

DES REFORMES POUR UNE SOCIETE VIEILLISSANTE (2000)

UN SYSTÈME DE COMPTES DE LA SANTÉ (2000)

Health Working Papers

Une nouvelle série destinée à rendre disponible à une plus grande audience les études de santé disséminées à l'OCDE. Disponibles en anglais seulement. Téléchargement gratuit sur www.oecd.org/els/health/workingpapers.

Les derniers numéros incluent :

Health-Care Systems: Lessons from the Reform Experience (OECD Health Working Papers No.9) Décembre 2003

Private Health Insurance in Australia: A Case Study (OECD Health Working Papers No.8) Octobre 2003

Explaining Waiting Times Variations for Elective Surgery across OECD Countries (OECD Health Working Paper No.7) Octobre 2003

Tackling Excessive Waiting Times for Elective Surgery: A Comparison of Policies in Twelve OECD Countries (OECD Health Working Paper No.6) Juillet 2003

Stroke Care in OECD Countries: A Comparison of Treatment, Costs and Outcomes in 17 Countries (OECD Health Working Papers NO.5) Juin 2003

Survey of Pharmacoeconomic Assessment Activity in Eleven Countries (OECD Health Working Paper NO.4) Mai 2003

OECD Study of Cross-National Differences in the Treatment, Costs and Outcomes of Ischaemic Heart Disease (OECD Health Working Paper NO.3) Avril 2003

Investment in Population Health in Five OECD Countries (OECD Health Working Paper N°2) Avril 2003

Pharmaceutical Use and Expenditure for Cardiovascular Disease and Stroke: a Study of 12 OECD Countries (OECD Health Working Papers No.1) Février 2003

Politique sociale - Documents hors-série dans le domaine de la santé

Disponibles pour téléchargement gratuit sur http://www.oecd.org/document/25/0,2340,en_2649_33929_2380441_1_1_1_1,00.html.

Les numéros les plus récents sont:

No. 57 IMPROVING THE PERFORMANCE OF HEALTH CARE SYSTEMS: FROM MEASURES TO ACTION (2001) Zeynep Or

No. 56 AN ASSESSMENT OF THE PERFORMANCE OF THE JAPANESE HEALTH CARE SYSTEM (2001) Hyoung-Sun Jeong et Jeremy Hurst

No. 53 TOWARDS MORE CHOICE IN SOCIAL PROTECTION? INDIVIDUAL CHOICE OF INSURER IN BASIC MANDATORY HEALTH INSURANCE IN SWITZERLAND (2001) Francesca Colombo

No. 47 PERFORMANCE MEASUREMENT AND PERFORMANCE MANAGEMENT IN OECD HEALTH SYSTEMS (2001) Jeremy Hurst et Melissa Jee-Hughes

Pour une liste complète des publications de l'OCDE,
veuillez consulter le site internet de la librairie de l'OCDE :
www.oecd.org/bookshop
ou nous écrire pour recevoir gratuitement le catalogue des publications à l'adresse suivante :
Service des Publications OCDE
2, rue André-Pascal,
75775 PARIS CEDEX 16

Français

OECD GESUNDHEITSDATEN 2004

VERGLEICHENDE ANALYSE VON 30 LÄNDERN

Deutsch

Benutzerhandbuch

OECD GESUNDHEITSDATEN 2004 wurde gemeinsam vom OECD-Sekretariat und dem französischen Forschungsinstitut IRDES (Institut de Recherche et d'Etude en Economie de la Santé) entwickelt.

Das OECD-Team setzte sich aus Gaëlle Balestat, Marie-Clémence Canaud, Manfred Huber, Gaetan Lafortune, David Morgan und Eva Orosz. Das IRDES -Team bestand aus Catherine Banchereau, Martine Broïdo, Jacques Harrouin, Christophe Lainé, Florence Naudin und Thierry Rochereau.

Für alle Fragen zu den Daten, Quellen, Methoden und Systemdarstellungen wenden Sie sich bitte an :	Für Fragen der technischen Unterstützung wenden Sie sich bitte an :
OECD Health Policy Unit 2, rue André Pascal F-75775 Paris Cedex 16 (Frankreich) Fax : (33) 1 44 30 63 61 E-mail : health.contact@oecd.org	**IRDES** 10, rue Vauvenargues F-75018 Paris (Frankreich) Fax : (33) 1 53 93 43 50 (zu Hd. Eco-Santé-Team) E-mail : ecosante@irdes.fr Web : www.irdes.fr

Häufig gestellte Fragen

Hinsichtlich häufig gestellter Fragen zur Version 2004 werden sich die OECD und das IRDES bemühen, rasch über ihre Internet-Sites zu antworten sowie Updates, Zusatzinformationen über die Variablen, Tabellenbeispiele und das voraussichtliche Erscheinungsdatum der OECD Gesundheitsdaten 2005 bereitzustellen.

- Bei technischen Problemen: www.irdes.fr/ecosante/faq.htm
- Zwecks Informationen und Updates: www.oecd.org/health/healthdata/

(Klicken Sie bitte auf **[Frequently Asked Questions]**).

Das Programmpaket OECD GESUNDHEITSDATEN 2004 umfasst :

- www.oecd.org/health/healthdata/
- www.irdes.fr/ecosante/index.htm

Das Programmpaket OECD GESUNDHEITSDATEN 2004 umfasst :

- eine CD-ROM mit den Programmdateien, Daten und Dienstprogrammen
- dieses Benutzerhandbuch

VORWORT

Die OECD GESUNDHEITSDATEN 2004, die hiermit in ihrer dreizehntes Fassung in Form einer elektronischen Datenbank über die Gesundheitssysteme vorliegen, beruhen auf mehr als fünfzehn Jahren Arbeit des OECD Sekretariats zu Gesundheitsstatistiken.

Nach über 15 Jahren der Sammlung statistischer Datenreihen hat die OECD dreizehn Versionen ihrer elektronischen Datenbank über Gesundheitssysteme fertig gestellt. Die Version 2004 enthält neue Daten und ein leistungsstärkeres Programm. Revidiert und ergänzt wurden auch die Standarddefinitionen der Variablen sowie die dazugehörigen Quellenangaben und die in den einzelnen Ländern verwendeten Methoden. Dank der Beiträge der Institutionen, von denen die Originaldaten stammen, bildet das Informationssystem eine wertvolle Hilfe zum besseren Verständnis der Trends sowie des Niveaus der Zeitreihen. Schließlich enthält die Version für Windows 98/2000/NT/Me/XP einige überarbeitete Funktionen als Weiterentwicklung dieser bewährten benutzerfreundlichen Software.

Besonderer Dank gilt der Centers for Medicare and Medicaid Services (CMS, ex HCFA)des Gesundheitsministeriums der Vereinigten Staaten für ihre finanzielle Unterstützung. Herzlich gedankt sei auch den hunderten von Statistikern aus den 30 Mitgliedstaaten, von denen die meisten Zahlen und sonstigen Angaben stammen, auf denen dieses Informationssystem beruht.

Deutsch

EINFÜHRUNG

OECD GESUNDHEITSDATEN 2004 ist eine interaktive Software zur Darstellung systematisch erfasster Daten zu einer großen Zahl unterschiedlicher Aspekte der Gesundheitssysteme der 30 OECD-Mitgliedstaaten zusammen mit ihrem demographischen, wirtschaftlichen und sozialen Kontext.

Die zehnte Ausgabe dieses benutzerfreundlichen Informationssystems ermöglicht es, OECD-Daten abzufragen, sie an Hand von Tabellen, Grafiken oder Karten zu analysieren und in andere Anwendungen zu exportieren. Variablen, Länder und Jahre können vom Benutzer beliebig ausgewählt werden. Die derzeit nahezu 1200 Datenreihen umspannen den Zeitraum 1960-2002, wobei für einige Variablen durchgehende Zeitreihen seit 1960 verfügbar sind. Die meisten Daten umfassen die achtziger und neunziger Jahre, oftmals bis 2001 oder 2002 und in einigen Fällen bis zum Jahr 2003.

Die *OECD GESUNDHEITSDATEN 2004* für Windows 98/2000/NT/Me/XP gibt es in vier Sprachfassungen (Französisch/Englisch/Deutsch/Spanisch). Sie sind das Ergebnis einer gemeinsamen Entwicklung von OECD und IRDES in einander ergänzenden Fachbereichen :

- Veröffentlichung und Aktualisierung statistischer Indikatoren zum Gesundheitswesen und der Wirtschaftspolitik in den 30 OECD-Mitgliedstaaten und

- Entwicklung einer Software mit volkswirtschaftlichen Daten zur Beschreibung der Funktionsweise von Gesundheitssystemen.

Dieses Benutzerhandbuch enthält Angaben über den Inhalt der Datenbank, die Analysefunktionen sowie über den praktischen Umgang mit der Software.

Neuheiten in der 2004 Version der *OECD Gesundheitsdaten*

Die *OECD GESUNDHEITSDATEN 2004* enthalten eine Reihe von Verbesserungen und NeuheitenNeuerungen:

- Neues Installationsverfahren;
- Neues Programmdesign im XP-Stil;
- Hinzufügung der Suchmerkmale "Schlüsselwörter" und "Volltext" im Hypertext für *Quellen und Methoden*, zusammen mit einem neuen Navigationsindex;
- Neue Export- und Druckoptionen für *Definitionen, Quellen und Methoden*;
- Programm und Variablenliste nun auch in russischer Sprache verfügbar;
- Verbesserte Funktionen zum Wechseln der Programmsprache (mit einem Klick erscheinen alle Angaben in der gleichen Sprache);
- Einbeziehung der vorläufigen Ergebnisse des OECD-Gesundheitsprojekts in den Hypertext.

> Die Datei LiesMich.txt dokumentiert in letzter Minute erfolgte Änderungen und Hinzufügungen und kann am Ende des Installationsvorgangs eingesehen werden. Um die Datei später zu lesen, klicken Sie einfach auf das Symbol LiesMich im Ordner OECD GESUNDHEITSDATEN 2004.

KAPITEL 1: INSTALLIEREN DER SOFTWARE

Erforderliche Hardwareausstattung und Systemkonfiguration

Zur Nutzung dieser Software sind folgende Grundvoraussetzungen nötig :

- Windows 98/2000/NT/Me/XP ;
- 64 MB RAM ;
- 70 MB freie Festplatten-Speicherkapazität ;
- CD-ROM-Laufwerk (nur für die Installation) ;
- Grafikkarte : 16 bits 800x600.

Sollte sich auf Ihrer Festplatte eine frühere *OECD-Gesundheitsdaten*-Version befinden, empfiehlt es sich, diese zu löschen, damit sie nicht unnötig Platz belegt. Um dies zu machen, wählen Sie den ikon Programm Addieren/Beseitigen (add/Remove Programs) im Control Panel. Hinweis: Vordefinierte Tabellen aus einer persönlich angelegten Bibliothekin in einer früheren Version der *OECD Gesundheitsdaten* sind nicht übertragbar.

Installieren der Software

Vor dem Installieren der Software sind alle aktiven Anwendungen zu schließen und etwaige Anti-Virus-Programme zu desaktivieren. Prüfen Sie bitte auch nach, ob Sie befugt sind, diese Software auf dem gewählten PC zu installieren. Wenden Sie sich ggf. an Ihren PC- oder Netzwerkadministrator.

Um Ihr Programm zu installieren, starten Sie Windows und legen Sie die CD-ROM in das Laufwerk ein. Ein gerahmter Abschnitt zeigt die Besonderheiten einer *OECD Gesundheitsdaten* installation für die **Netzwerk-Version** an.

CD-Rom wird nur für die Installation benötigt :

Klicken Sie auf die Schaltfläche **[Starten]** und wählen Sie **[Ausführen]** ;

Schreiben Sie auf der Zeile **[Öffnen]** "d:\install", wobei d: Ihr CD-ROM-Laufwerk bezeichnet (auch andere Laufwerksbezeichnungen können verwendet werden) ;

Bestätigen Sie Ihre Wahl mit **[OK]**.

Falls Ihr CD-ROM-Laufwerk auf **[AutoBoot]** programmiert ist, läuft die Installation des *OECD Gesundheitsdaten* programms nach dem Einlegen der CD-ROM in das Laufwerk automatisch ab.

Ablauf der Installation :

- Wählen Sie die Sprache der Installation: Deutsch, Englisch, Französisch, Spanisch ;
- Anschließend müssen Sie als Benutzer dem Nutzungsvertrag zustimmen ;
- Dann ist die Nutzerinformation und die CD-ROM-Seriennummer einzugeben einzugeben, **welche auf der Inneneabdeckung** dieses Benutzerhandbuches zu finden ist. Bei richtiger Eingabe läuft die Installation weiter ab. Andernfalls erfolgt eine Fehlermeldung und die Seriennummer muss von neuem eingegeben werden ;

- Wählen Sie das Verzeichnis in welchem das Programm installiert werden soll. Die Installationsroutine überprüft nun, ob ausreichend freier Speicherplatz verfügbar ist. Ist dies nicht der Fall, folgt die Aufforderung, Speicherkapazität frei zu geben oder das Verzeichnis zu wechseln ;
- Bestätigen Sie im letzten Fenster die Parameter der Installation, die anschließend automatisch abläuft.

Nach beendeter Installation erscheint ein Ordner mit den nötigen Symbolen zur Verzendung der *OECD GESUNDHEITSDATEN 2004.*

In einem Fenster werden dann für Fragen zur Software zweckdienliche Kontaktadressen sowie die Adressen der OECD- und IRDES-Internet-Sites angegeben.

NB: Die Installationsroutine fordert Sie in einigen Fällen auf, Ihren Rechner nach der Installation neu zu starten.

BESONDERHEITEN BEI DER INSTALLATION DER NETZWERK-VERSION DER *OECD GESUNDHEITSDATEN 2004*

Für die Installation der Netzwerk-Version hat der Netzwerkadministrator zunächst die Server-Seite der Software zu installieren. Diese Installation ist identisch mit der oben beschriebenen Installation der Einzelplatzversion. Der entsprechende Pfad muss für alle potentiellen Benutzer zugänglich sein.

Dann ist auf jedem Einzelplatz die Client-Seite der Software zu installieren. Das entsprechende Installationsprogramm **install.exe** befindet sich im Unterverzeichnis **USER**.

Wurde die Server-Seite beispielsweise auf dem Pfad E:\APPLIK\ECOSANTE2004 installiert, so befindet sich das Installationsprogramm der Client-Seite unter E:\APPLIK\ECOSANTE2004\USER\ INSTALL.EXE.

Das Verzeichnis c:\ecowin2004 wird automatisch vom Installationsprogramm der Client-Seite erstellt. Falls Sie das c Nutzerverzeichnis an einer anderen Stelle wünschen, müssen Sie auch den Parameter LocalPath in der Datei Ecowin.ini im Windows-Verzeichnis ändern.

Vom Nutzer abgespeicherte Dateien werden, falls nicht anders angegeben, automatisch im lokalen Verzeichnis c:\ecowin2004\result abgelegt. Damit hat jeder Nutzer die Möglichkeit, über eigene Ländergruppen und gespeicherte Tabellen zu verfügen.

Die Installation auf der Server-Seite belegt weniger als 1 MB Speicherplatz auf der lokalen Platte

---

Starten des Programms

Wählen Sie **[Starten - Programme - OECD-GESUNDHEITSDATEN 2004]** und klicken Sie dann auf **[OECD-Gesundheitsdaten]**.

Für einen einwandfreien Betrieb sind auf der Festplatte nach Installation der Software mindestens 5 MB freie Speicherkapazität erforderlich, um Arbeits- und Sicherungsdateien ablegen zu können.

Zur Erkundung der verschiedenen Möglichkeiten, die die Software bietet, lassen Sie sich nach Orientierung an Hand der Erläuterungstexte von den einzelnen Informationsfenstern leiten.

Bei der ersten Benutzung der Software blenden sich automatisch Infoblasen (siehe unten) ein. Dennoch empfehlen wir Ihnen, sich mit dem Inhalt dieses Benutzerhandbuches vertraut zu machen, bevor Sie mit der Software zu arbeiten beginnen.

Entfernen des Programms

Um die *OECD GESUNDHEITSDATEN 2004* aus Ihrem System zu entfernen verlassen Sie das programm (Programs). Klicken Sie auf die Schaltfläche **[Starten]** (Start), whälen Sie **[Einstellungen]** (Settings). Whälen Sie den Ikon Programm **[Addieren/Beseitigen]** (Add/Remove Programs) im Control Panel. Whälen Sie **[OECD GESUNDHEITSDATEN 2004]** von der Liste und klicken Sie **[Addieren/Beseitigen]** (Add/Remove). Klicken Sie OK, um die Desinstallation des Programs zu bestätigen.

Die CD-ROM ist zum Löschen des Programms nicht erforderlich.

Aktualisieren der Daten via Internet

Nach der Veröffentlichung des OECD-Gesundheitsdaten programms werden etwaige Verbesserungen in den Dateien und Hinzufügungen durch kostenlose Updates bereitgestellt. Machen Sie von der Möglichkeit Gebrauch, Ihre Daten über Internet zu aktualisieren.

Internet :

* Schalten Sie sich auf eine der folgenden Websites :

  ⇨ OECD-Site: www.oecd.org/health/healthdata ;

  ⇨ IRDES-Site: www.irdes.fr/ecosante/index.htm ;

* OECD-Site: auf **[Updates]** klicken; IRDES-Site: auf **[Mise à jour des données]** klicken ;

* Doppelklicken Sie auf **[Chargement]** bzw. **[Download]** und geben Sie das Verzeichnis in Ihrem PC an, in das Sie die Dateien kopieren wollen ;

Unter Windows :

* Nach Laden der aktualisierten Datei doppelklicken. Sie zum Entpackenauf das Symbol (oder den Dateinamen) ;

* Überspielt wird eine komprimierte, selbstextrahierende Datei (.EXE), die zwei Einzeldateien enthält :

  ⇨ Aktualisierte Datenbank ;

  ⇨ LiesMich-Datei mit Erläuterung der Neuerungen in der aktualisierten Datei.

* Geben Sie den Namen des Dateiordners ein, in dem Sie Ihre Datenbank OECD Gesundheitsdaten 2004 (z.B. c:\software\ecowin2004) installiert haben und klicken Sie auf OK, um die Eingabe zu bestätigen;

* Bei Unmittelbar vor Beginn des Aktualisierungsprozesses erscheint ein Fenster, in dem der Titel der Datenbank und die aktuelle Version angezeigt werden (z.B., OECD Gesundheitsdaten 2004, Vers.2): Klicken Sie auf " Start update ", um den Aktualisierungsprozess zu lancieren.

* Sollte das Update nicht starten, prüfen Sie bitte sorgfältig den Namen des Dateiordners , in dem Sie die Datenbank installiert haben und geben Sie diesen erneut ein.

Im Hauptfenster der OECD Gesundheitsdaten 2004:

Nach erfolgreicher Aktualisierung, haben sich Datum und Name derVersion unter dem Titel "OECD GESUNDHEITSDATEN 2004" verändertgeändert.

Hauptfenster der OECD GESUNDHEITSDATEN 2004

Die einzelnen Funktionen werden über Schaltflächen aktiviert. Durch einfaches Klicken wird entweder die der Schaltfläche zugeordnete Funktion sofort ausgeführt, oder es erscheint ein Dialogfeld zur Auswahl verschiedener Parameter, bevor der Befehl ausgeführt wird.

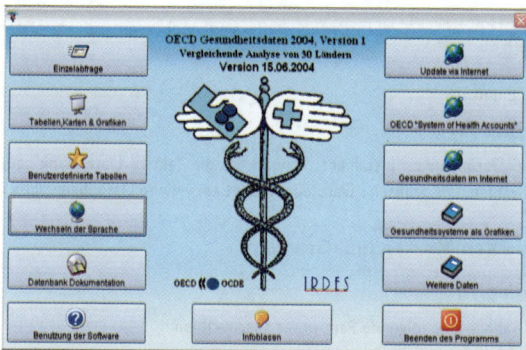

[Einzelabfrage] dient zur Auswahl einer Variablen, um die entsprechenden Werte für ein oder alle angegebenen Länder für ein, zwei oder alle verfügbaren Jahre abzufragen und die Veränderungsraten im Bezugszeitraum zu berechnen. Mit dieser Funktion können Sie auch Karten erstellen sowie Tabellen ausdrucken oder exportieren.

[Tabellen, Karten & Grafiken] dient zur Auswahl von einer oder mehreren Variablen, um die entsprechenden Werte für ein oder mehrere Länder für ein oder mehrere Jahre abzufragen und die Veränderungsraten im Bezugszeitraum zu berechnen. Mit dieser Funktion können Sie auch Karten und Grafiken erstellen.

Klicken Sie auf **[Tabellen Gespeichert]**, um zuvor erstellte bzw. Von der OECD vordefinierte Tabellen aufzurufen. Damit können Sie Ihre eigene Tabellenbibliothek abspeichern.

[Wechseln der Sprache] dient zur Auswahl der gewünschten Arbeitssprache für die Benutzerführung (Englisch, Französisch, Deutsch oder Spanisch) sowie die Variablen-(Englisch bzw. Französisch).

Klicken Sie auf **[Datenbank Dokumentation]** um den Index der Variablen-Info aufzurufen, um die zugeordneten Bezugsdefinitionen, Quellen und Methoden einzusehen.

Klicken Sie auf **[Beenden des Programms]** um die Arbeitssitzung abzuschliessen.

Klicken Sie auf **[Benutzung der Software]** um den Zugang zum Inhaltsverzeichnis der Online-Hilfe des Programms zu erhalten.

Klicken Sie auf **[Infoblasen]** um die Erläuterungen zu den Schaltflächen und Programmobjekten ein- bzw. auszublenden.

Direkter Internet-Zugriff : Schaltflächen mit diesem Logo bieten direkten Zugang zu den OECD Websites mit Gesundheitsdaten, auch der Seite für das Herunterladen von Internet-Aktualisierungen.

Hilfe

Variablen-Info: Quellen und Methoden

Für die den Variablen zugeordneten Quellen und Methoden steht Ihnen eine kontextsensitive Hilfe und ein Hilfe-Index zur Verfügung.

Für den Zugriff zur kontextsensitiven Hilfe klicken Sie mit der rechten Maustaste auf die Variable, für die Sie die Bezugsdefinition, Quelle und/oder Abweichung gegenüber der Bezugsdefinition nachschlagen wollen. In den *OECD GESUNDHEITSDATEN 2004* wird eine solche Hilfe in den Listenfeldern Kapitel und Variablen geboten.

Für den Zugriff zum allgemeinen Hilfe-Index der Variablen-Info (Quellen und Methoden) klicken Sie, falls vorhanden, auf die Schaltfläche **[Quellen]**. Wählen Sie dann das Kapitel und die Variable, über die Sie Informationen wünschen.

Abgesehen von den *OECD GESUNDHEITSDATEN 2004* sind noch zwei weitere Datenbanken bei IRDES erhältlich :

- Eco-Santé FRANCE und
- Eco-Santé REGIONAL (Frankreich)

Sind mindestens zwei Datenbanken installiert, können Sie die "aktive Datenbank" aus der zugeordneten Dropdown-Liste auswählen. Die grafische Darstellung zeigt an, welche Datenbank aktiv ist.

Erstellen von Tabellen, Karten und Grafiken

Auswahl einer Variablen

Zur Erstellung einer Tabelle sind folgende Parameter auszuwählen :

- aus dem Register Kapitel der Eintrag, zu dem die gewünschte Variable gehört (z.B. Gesundheitsberufe) ;
- aus dem Register Variable eine der Variablen, die dem Kapitel zugeordnet ist (z.B. Praktizierende Apotheker) ;
- aus dem Register Einheit eine der aufgelisteten Einheiten (z.B. Zahl je 1000 Einwohner).

Klicken Sie im **"Variable"**-Register auf die Schaltfläche **[Hinzu]** bzw. auf das leere Register-Feld, um die Liste der Variablen anzuzeigen.

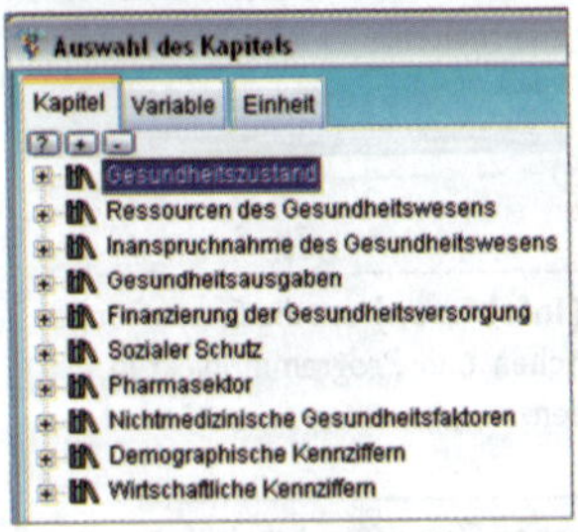

- Die Bezeichnungen der einzelnen Kapitel, Variablen und Einheiten erscheinen in abgekürzter, jedoch ausreichend verständlicher Form.
- Die miteinander logisch verknüpften Daten führen in einfacher Schrittfolge zur gewünschten Variablen. Außerdem können Sie in der Liste der Variablen in Kapitel 3 nachsehen.

Im Register **"Kapitel"** stehen drei Schaltflächen zur Verfügung: 

Durch Klicken auf **[+]** werden für alle Kapitel sämtliche Unterkapitel angezeigt.
Durch Klicken auf **[-]** wird die Auflistung der untergeordneten Ebenen geschlossen.

Mehrfachauswahl

Um Variable auszuwählen, die mehreren Kapiteln gemeinsam sind,bietet die Software eine Art Schnellverfahren. Allerdings wird dabei vorausgesetzt, dass der Inhalt der betreffenden Kapitel bekannt ist.

Markieren Sie durch Klicken das Feld **[Mehrfachauswahl]**. Markieren Sie durch Klicken auf die vor den Kapitelnamen erscheinenden Felder diejenigen Kapitel, die die gesuchten Variablen enthalten.

Nach Beendigung der Kapitelauswahl klicken Sie auf **[weiter]**, um das Fenster zur Variablenauswahl aufzurufen. In diesem Fenster erscheinen nur diejenigen Variablen, die den zuvor ausgewählten Kapiteln gemeinsam sind. Für die weiteren Schritte (Auswahl einer oder mehrerer Variablen, Auswahl einer oder mehrerer Einheiten) siehe oben.

Auswahl der Länder

Klicken Sie zur Auswahl der Länder auf das Register **"Länder"**.

Das obere linke Fenster enhält die Liste der 30 OECD-Mitgliedstaaten; das untere linke Fenster zeigt die Ländergruppen. Das rechte Fenster dient zur Anzeige der gewählten Länder.

Auswahl eines oder mehrerer Länder

Klicken Sie zur Auswahl eines Landes

- entweder zweimal auf das gewünschte Land
- oder einmal auf das Land und dann auf die Schaltfläche **[+]**.

Klicken Sie zur Wahl aller Länder auf die Schaltfläche **[++]**. Damit werden alle Länder in das rechte Fenster übertragen.

Zum Entfernen von einem bzw. allen Ländern klicken Sie auf die Schaltfläche **[-]** bzw. **[--]**.

Systembeschreibungen

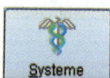

Der Aufruf der Systembeschreibungen erfolgt entweder kontextsensitiv oder über den allgemeinen Index. Diese beschreiben für die meisten OECD-Staaten in Form von Grafiken die Wechselbeziehungen zwischen Finanzierung und Leistungserbringung.
Der Zugriff zur kontextsensitiven Hilfe erfolgt durch Klicken mit dem rechten Mausknopf auf das Land, über das Sie Näheres wissen möchten.
Der Zugriff zum allgemeinen Index der *Systeme* erfolgt durch Klicken auf die Schaltfläche **[Systeme]**. Wählen Sie dann im Index das Land, über das Sie sich informieren wollen.

Auswahl der Jahre und Zeiträume

Klicken Sie auf das Register **"Jahre und Zeiträume"**, um die Jahre und Zeiträume zur Berechnung der Veränderungsraten auszuwählen.

Die linke Spalte "Verfügbare Jahre" zeigt sämtliche Jahre an, für die Daten verfügbar sind. Da für einzelne Variablen nicht immer Daten für alle Jahre in allen Ländern verfügbar sind, haben Sie durch Klicken auf die Schaltfläche **[Verfügbarkeit]** unten rechts die Möglichkeit, dies nachzuprüfen.

blau = Jahre, für die Daten verfügbar sind
grün = gewählte Jahre

Ergebnisanzeige

Vor Anzeige der Tabelle erscheint der nachstehende Hinweis, um Sie auf die darauf aufmerksam zu machen, dass beim Variablenvergleich zwischen verschiedenen Ländern Vorsicht geboten ist.

Deutsch

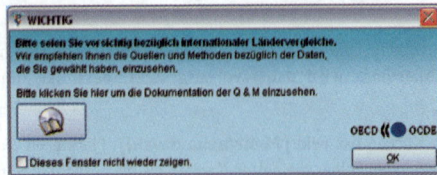

Zur Anzeige der Tabelle auf **[OK]** klicken.

Tabellen-Symbolleiste

Verkleinert/vergrößert die Symbolleiste.

100% ▼ Verkleinert/vergrößert das aktive Spreadsheet.

Justiert automatisch die Spaltenbreite. Bildet je nach Inhalt unterschiedlich breite Spalten.

Bildet gleich breite Spalten nach dem Vorbild der aktiven Spalte.

Aktiviert/deaktiviert die Gitternetzlinien.

Aktiviert/deaktiviert das Legendenfenster.

Sortiert die Tabelleneinträge in der aktiven Spalte in aufsteigender bzw. abnehmender Reihenfolge.

Fügt nach Angabe von Position und Inhalt eine neue Spalte hinzu.

Löschen der betreffenden Spalte nach Eingabe der Spaltenposition. Falls nicht anders angegeben, wird die aktive Spalte gelöscht.

Errechnet einen Vergleichsindex.

Addiert eine Spalte, um Ranking darzustellen.

Arithmetisches Mittel der Werte der aktiven Spalte (Ergebnisanzeige in der letzten Zeile).

Summe der Werte der aktiven Spalte (Ergebnisanzeige in der letzten Zeile).

Öffnen des Druckeinstellfensters.

Öffnen des Tabellenexportfensters.

Kopieren des markierten Bereichs in die Zwischenablage und Einfügen in eine andere Windows-Anwendung (mit der Option **[Einfügen]** des Menüs Bearbeiten oder mit der Tastenkombination **[STRG+V]**).

Zugriff zum Grafikmodul.

Erstellen einer Karte ausgehend von der aktiven Spalte, sofern die Zeilen der Tabelle Länder darstellen.

Zugriff zur Programm-Hilfe.

Zugriff zur Variablenbeschreibung (Quellen und Methoden).

Schließen des Tabellenansichtfensters.

Zum Ändern der Spaltenüberschrift doppelklicken Sie auf den entsprechenden Titel. Zum Ändern der Tabellenüberschrift doppelklicken Sie auf das leere Feld, das sich auf der Tabelle oben links befindet.

Alle Symbolleisten-Funktionen können direkt mittels Mausklick (rechte Taste) auf dem Titel einer Spalte in einer Tabelle ausgeführt werden. Ein Mausklick (ebenfalls mit der rechten Taste) auf dem Titel eines Indikators (mit Variablen in den Zeilen und Jahren oder Ländern in den Spalten) liefert die entsprechenden Definitionen, Quellen- und Methodenangaben.

Exportieren von Tabellen

Zum Exportieren der Tabelle klicken Sie auf das entsprechende Feld in der Symbolleiste des **Tabellenansichtfensters**.

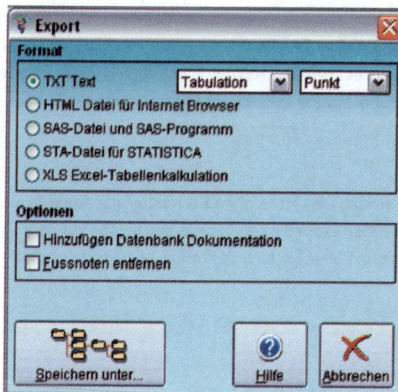

Sie können unter fünf Exportarten wählen :

- **Text.TXT**

Exportmodus : Textdatei. Dabei ist die gewünschte Spaltentrennung (Tabulation, Leerstelle, Komma, Strichpunkt) und das Dezimalzeichen (Punkt bzw. Komma) festzulegen.

- **SAS-System**

Beim Exportieren einer Tabelle im SAS-Format werden zwei Dateien erzeugt, eine erste mit den Daten (mit der Erweiterung ".DAT") und eine zweite mit einer Beschreibung der Variablen und einer Gliederung der Daten (mit der Erweiterung ".SAS"). Zum Importieren dieser Datei in die SAS-Software wählen Sie "Programm ausführen". Ausgehend von der Datendatei erstellt das Programm ein temporäres SAS-Verzeichnis (Work). Damit kann das Ergebnis in einer SAS-Umgebung eingesehen werden. (Mehr Informationen über das SAS-System siehe: www.sas.com/).

Klicken Sie zur Festlegung des Speicherpfads auf **[Speichern unter]**. Es erscheint ein Fenster mit Angabe des Vorgabeverzeichnisses, in dem Ihre Dateien abgelegt werden.

Wählen Sie mit dem Windows-üblichen Verfahren das gewünschte Verzeichnis, in dem Sie Ihre Dateien ablegen wollen.

Geben Sie der Datei auf der Zeile "Datei" einen Namen. Falls nicht anders angegeben, wird die für das Exportformat gewählte Erweiterung herangezogen.

Klicken Sie auf die Schaltfläche **[Speichern]**. Die Meldung "Datei gespeichert" informiert Sie über den einwandfreien Ablauf des Exportiervorgangs.

Klicken Sie auf **[Abbrechen]**, um zum **"Exportfenster"** zurückzukehren.

- **STA-Datei für STATISTICA**

Mit diesem Format wird eine Datei mit der Erweiterung .STA für die statistische Software STATISTICA des Softwarehauses StatSoft (www.statsoft.com/) erstellt. In der erstellten Datei erscheinen der Tabellentitel, die Reihen sowie die Bezeichnungen der Variablen.

- **HTML**

Mit diesem Format können Sie eine Tabelle erstellen, die mit Hilfe eines Internet-Navigationssystems wie Netscape oder Internet Explorer angezeigt werden kann. Vorteil dieses Formats ist, dass die Dateien aufallen Rechnern (PC, Macintosh, Unix Station etc.) direkt angezeigt werden können.

- **Excel.XLS**

Mit diesem Exportmodus werden die Daten ohne Konvertierung direkt in eine Excel-Datei, Version 4.0 und höher, übertragen. Die Titel der exportierten Tabelle erscheinen auf dem Excel-Spreadsheet in einer Zelle oben links. (Mehr Informationen über Excel: http://office.microsoft.com/home/default.aspx).

Grafikmodul

Das Grafikmodul ist verbessert worden: Diagramme lassen sich nun direkt in der Datentabelle erstellen. Das Diagrammmenü hat eine eigene Hilfefunktion.

TEIL I - GESUNDHEITSZUSTAND

Mortalität

Lebenserwartung

Frauen bei der Geburt
Frauen im Alter von 40 Jahren
Frauen im Alter von 60 Jahren
Frauen im Alter von 65 Jahren
Frauen im Alter von 80 Jahren
Männer bei der Geburt
Männer im Alter von 40 Jahren
Männer im Alter von 60 Jahren
Männer im Alter von 65 Jahren
Männer im Alter von 80 Jahren
Bei der Geburt

Todesursachen

Alle Kategorien
Infektiöse und parasitäre Krankheiten.
HIV-Virus (AIDS)
Bösartige Neubildungen
Bösartige Neubildung des Colons
Bösartige Neubildung der Lunge
Bösartige Neubildung der weiblichen Brust
Bösartige Neubildung der Cervix
Bösartige Neubildung der Prostata
Blutkrankheiten
Endokrinopathien, Ernährungs-und Stoffwechselkrankheit
Diabetes mellitus
Psychiatrische Krankheiten
Krankheiten des Nervensystems
Krankheiten des Kreislaufsystems
Ischämische Herzkrankheiten
Akuter Myokardinfarkt
Zerebrovaskuläre Krankheiten
Krankheiten der Atmungsorgane
Grippe und Pneumonie
Bronchitis, Asthma, Emphysem
Krankheiten der Verdauungsorgane

Chronische Leberkrankheiten und Zirrhose
Krankheiten der Haut und des subkutanen Gewebes
Muskel- und Skeletterkrankungen
Krankheiten der Harn- und Geschlechtsorgane
Kr. Skelett+Muskeln+Bindegewebe
Krkht. Harn- u. Geschlechtsorgane
Schwangerschaft, Geburt und Wochenbett
Perinatale Affektionen
Kongenitale Anomalien
Symptome & mangelhaft bezeichnete Krankheiten
Externe Todesursachen
Kraftfahrzeugunfälle
Unfälle durch Sturz
Absichtliche, sich selbst zugefügte Verletzung
Tätlicher Angriff
Unerwünschte Nebenwirkungen von Arzneimitteln
Medizinische oder chirurgische Komplikationen

Mutter-Kind Mortalität

Säuglings-/Kleinkindsterblichkeit
Neonatale Mortalität
Perinatale Mortalität
Maternale Mortalität

Potentiell yerlorene Lebensjahre

Alle Kategorien
Infektiöse und parasitäre Krankheiten
HIV-Virus (AIDS)
Bösartige Neubildungen
Bösartige Neubildung des Colons
Bösartige Neubildung des Lunge
Bösartige Neubildung der weiblichen Brust
Bösartige Neubildung der Cervix
Bösartige Neubildung der Prostata
Blutkrankheiten
Endokrinopathien, Ernährungs-und Stoffwechselkrankheit.
Diabetes mellitus

Deutsch

Psychiatrische Krankheiten
Krankheiten des Nervensystems
Krankheiten des Kreislaufsystems
Ischämische Herzkrankheiten
Akuter Myokardinfarkt
Zerebrovaskuläre Krankheiten
Krankheiten der Atmungsorgane
Grippe und Pneumonie
Bronchitis, Asthma, Emphysem
Krankheiten der Verdauungsorgane
Chronische Leberkrankheiten/Zirrhose
Krankheiten der Haut und des subkutanen Gewebes
Muskel- und Skeletterkrankungen
Krankheiten der Harn- und Geschlechtsorgane
Schwangerschaft, Geburt und Wochenbett
Perinatale Affektionen
Kongenitale Anomalien
Symptome und mangelhaft bezeichnete Krankheiten
Externe Todesursachen
Kraftfahrzeugunfälle
Unfälle durch Sturz
Absichtliche, sich selbst zugefügte Verletzung
Tätlicher Angriff
Unerwünschte Nebenwirkungen von Arzneimitteln
Medizinische oder chirurgische Komplikationen

Morbidität

Selbsteinschätzung des Gesundheitszustandes

Gesundheit ≥ gut, Frauen 15-24
Gesundheit ≥ gut, Frauen, 25-44
Gesundheit ≥ gut, Frauen, 45-64
Gesundheit ≥ gut, Frauen, 65+
Gesundheit ≥ gut, Frauen, alle Altersstufen
Gesundheit ≥ gut, Männer, 15-24
Gesundheit ≥ gut, Männer, 25-44
Gesundheit ≥ gut, Männer, 45-64
Gesundheit ≥ gut, Männer 65+
Gesundheit ≥ gut, Männer alle Altersstufen
Gesundheit ≥ gut, gesamt, 15-24
Gesundheit ≥ gut, gesamt, 25-44
Gesundheit ≥ gut, gesamt, 45-64
Gesundheit ≥ gut, gesamt, 65+
Gesundheit ≥ gut, gesamt, alle Altersstufen

Kinder- und Säuglingsgesundheit

Untergewicht bei Geburt

Kongenitale Anomalien

Spina bifida
Transposition der großen Gefäße
Angeb. Missbild. Gliedmaßen
Down-Syndrom

Zahnmedizin

Kariöse, fehlende, plombierte Zähne

Übertragbare Krankheiten

Erworbenes Immunschwächesyndrom (AIDS)

Krebs

Bösartige Neubildungen
Bösartige Neubildung des Colons
Bösartige Neubildung der Lunge
Bösartige Neubildung weibl. Brust
Bösartige Neubildung d. Cervix
Bösartige Neubildung der Prostata

Unfälle

Verletzte durch Verkehrsunfälle

Fehlzeiten durch Krankheit

Fehlzeiten durch Krankheit (Umfragedaten)
Fehlzeiten durch Krankheit (erstattet)

TEIL 2 - RESSOURCEN DES GESUNDHEITSWESENS

Gesundheitsberufe

Gesundheitsberufe insgesamt
Krankenhauspersonal insgesamt
Praktizierende Ärzte
Praktizierende Ärzte: weiblich
Praktizierende Allgemeinärzte
Praktizierende Fachärzte
Praktizierende Zahnärzte
Praktizierende Apotheker
Krankenschwestern/Pfleger

Krankenhausbetten

Betten: akute station. Versorgung
Betten: Pflegeheime

Verhältnis Beschäftigte/Betten

Krankenhauspersonal für akute stationäre Versorgung
Pflegekräfte für akute stationäre Versorgung

Medizintechnik

Computer-Tomographen
Magnetresonanz-Tomographie
Röntgentherapiegeräte
Lithotripter
Hämodialysestationen
Mammographen

Verhältnis Beschäftigte/Betten

Personal: akute stat. Versorgung
Pflegekräfte: akute stat. Versorg.

Ausbildung zu Gesundheitsberufen

Absolventen Medizin, ISCED 3
Absolventen Medizin, ISCED 4
Absolventen Medizin, ISCED 5A
Absolventen Medizin, ISCED 5B
Absolventen Medizin, ISCED 6

TEIL 3 - INANSPRUCHNAHME VON RESSOURCEN

Prävention (Impfschutz)

Impfschutz: Diphteria,Tetanus, Pertussis
Impfschutz: Masern
Impfschutz: Grippe

Konsultationen

Arztbesuche
Zahnarztbesuche

Inanspruchnahme der stationären Versorgung

Pflegetage: akute stat. Versorg.
Belegungsquote: akute stat. Vers.
Bettenumschlag: ak. stat. Versorg.

Mittlere Verweildauer

Mittlere Verweildauer: stationäre und akute Versorgung

Mittlere Verweildauer: stationäre Versorgung
Mittlere Verweildauer: akute Versorgung

Mittlere Verweildauer: ICD

Alle Kategorien
Infektiöse und parasitäre Krankheiten
HIV-Virus (AIDS)

Bösartige Neubildungen
Bösartige Neubildung des Colons
Bösartige Neubildung der Lunge
Bösartige Neubildung der weiblichen Brust
Bösartige Neubildung der Prostata
Blutkrankheiten
Endokrinopathien, Ernährungs-und Stoffwechselkrankheit.
Diabetes mellitus
Krankheiten des Nervensystems
Seniler Katarakt
Otitis media
Krankheiten des Kreislaufsystems
Ischämische Herzkrankheiten
Akuter Myokardinfarkt
Zerebrovaskuläre Krankheiten
Krankheiten der Atmungsorgane
Grippe und Pneumonie
Bronchitis, Asthma, Emphysem
Krankheiten der Verdauungsorgane
Ulcus
Appendizitis
Leisten- und Schenkelbruch
Chronische Leberkrankheiten/Zirrhose
Cholelithiasis
Krankheiten der Haut und des subkutanen Gewebes
Muskel- und Skeletterkrankungen
Osteoarthrose
Diskopathien
Osteoporose
Krankheiten der Harn- und Geschlechtsorgane
Schwangerschaft, Geburt und Wochenbett
Normale Entbindung
Perinatale Affektionen
Kongenitale Anomalien
Symptome und mangelhaft bezeichnete Krankheiten
Externe Todesursachen
Oberschenkelhalsbruch
Sonstige Kategorien

Krankenhausfälle

Krankenhausfälle: ICD

Alle Kategorien
Infektiöse und parasitäre Krankheiten
HIV-Virus (AIDS)
Bösartige Neubildungen

Deutsch

Bösartige Neubildung des Colons
Bösartige Neubildung der Lunge
Bösartige Neubildung der weiblichen Brust
Bösartige Neubildung der Prostata
Blutkrankheiten
Endokrinopathien, Ernährungs-und Stoffwechselkrankheit.
Diabetes mellitus
Krankheiten des Nervensystems
Seniler Katarakt
Otitis media
Krankheiten des Kreislaufsystems
Ischämische Herzkrankheiten
Akuter Myokardinfarkt
Zerebrovaskuläre Krankheiten
Krankheiten der Atmungsorgane
Grippe und Pneumonie
Bronchitis, Asthma, Emphysem
Krankheiten der Verdauungsorgane
Ulcus
Appendizitis
Leisten- und Schenkelbruch
Chronische Leberkrankheiten/Zirrhose
Cholelithiasis
Krankheiten der Haut und des subkutanen Gewebes
Muskel- und Skeletterkrankungen
Osteoarthrose
Diskopathien
Osteoporose
Krankheiten der Harn- und Geschlechtsorgane
Schwangerschaft, Geburt und Wochenbett
Normale Entbindung
Perinatale Affektionen
Kongenitale Anomalien
Symptome und mangelhaft bezeichnete Krankheiten
Externe Todesursachen
Oberschenkelhalsbruch
Sonstige Kategorien

Chirurgische und ärztliche Eingriffe

Chirurgie insgesamt
Chirurgie insgesamt (stationäre und ambulant)
Stationäre Fälle
Ambulante Fälle

Chirurgische und ärztliche Eingriffe: ICD-CM
Kataraktextraktion
Tonsillektomie mit/ohne Adenoidektomie
Perkutane transluminale Koronarangioplastie
Koronarstent
Koronar-Bypass
Herzkatheterisierung
Herzschrittmacher
Venenresektion und Venenstripping
Appendektomie
Cholezystektomie
Laparoskopische Cholezystektomie
Leisten- und Schenkelbruch
Prostatektomie (transurethrale)
Prostatektomie (nicht transurethrale)
Hysterektomie (nur vaginal)
Kaiserschnitt
Hüftprothesen
Knie-prothesen
Brusterhaltende Chirurgie
Mastektomie

Transplantationen und Dialysen
Knochenmarktransplantation
Herztransplantation
Lebertransplantation
Lungentransplantation
Nierentransplantation
Funktionierende Nierentransplantate
Patienten mit termiinaler Niereninsuffizienz
Dialysepatienten
Heimdialysepatienten

TEIL 4 - GESUNDHEITSAUSGABEN

Nationale Gesundheitsausgaben

Gesamtgesundheitsausgaben
Gesamtgesundheitsausgaben
Laufende Gesamtgesundheitsausgaben
Gsmt.ausgaben für Investitionen für medizinische Einrichtungen
Öffentliche Gesundheitsausgaben
Laufende öffentliche Gesundheitsausgaben
Öffentliche Ausgaben für Investitionen für medizinische Einrichtungen
Private Gesundheitsausgaben

Laufende private Gesundheitsausgaben

Private Investitionen für medizinische Einrichtungen

Ausgaben für individuelle Gesundheitsversorgung

Gesamtausgaben individuelle Gesundheitsversorgung

Öffentliche Ausgaben für individuelle Gesundheitsvers.

Private Ausgaben für individuelle Gesundheitsversorung

Ausgaben für kollektive Gesundheitsversorgung

Gesamtausgaben für kollektive Gesundheitsversorgung

Öffentliche Ausgaben für kollektive Gesundheitsversorgung

Private Ausgaben für kollektive Gesundheitsversorgung

Prävention und Volksgesundheit

Gesamtausgaben für Prävention & öffentliche Gesundheit

Öffentliche Ausgaben für Prävention & öffentl. Gesundheit

Private Ausgaben für Prävention & öffentliche Gesundheit.

Ausgaben für Administration und Versicherung

Gesamtausgaben für Administration & Versicherung

Öffentliche Ausgaben für Administration & Versicherung

Private Ausgaben für Administration & Versicherung

Ausgaben für Gesundheit im weitesten Sinne

Ausgaben für Aus-und Weiterbildung von Gesundheitspersonal

Gesamtausgaben für F&E Gesundheit

Öffentliche Ausgaben für F&E Gesundheit

Ausgaben für medizinische Leistungen

Ausgaben für medizinische Leistungen nach Funktionen geord.

Gesamtausgaben für medizinische Leistungen

Gesamtausgaben für kurative & rehabilitative Leistungen

Gesamtausgaben für Langzeitpflege

Gesamtausgaben für sonstige Leistungen

Gesamtausgaben für Dienstleistungen: ohne Angabe der Funk.

Öffentliche Ausgaben für medizinische Leistungen

Öffentliche Ausgaben kurative & rehabilitative Leistungen

Öffentliche Ausgaben für Langzeitpflege

Öffentliche Ausgaben für sonstige Leistungen

Öffentliche Ausgaben für Dienstleistungen: ohne Angabe der Funk.

Private Ausgaben für medizinische Leistungen

Private Ausgaben für kurative & rehabilitative Leistungen

Private Ausgaben für Langzeitpflege

Private Ausgaben für sonstige Leistungen

Private Ausgaben für Dienstleistungen: ohne Angabe der Funk

Ausgaben für stationäre Leistungen

Gesamtausgaben stationäre Leistungen

Gesamtausgaben kurative & rehabilitative stationäre Leistungen

Gesamtausgaben für stationäre Langzeitpflege

Öffentliche Ausgaben für stationäre Leistungen

Öffentliche Ausgaben für kurative & rehabilitative stationäre Leistungen

Öffentliche Ausgaben für stationäre Langzeitpflege

Private Ausgaben für stationäre Leistungen

Private Ausgaben für kurative & rehabilitative stationäre Leistungen

Private Ausgaben für stationäre Langzeitpflege

Ausgaben für Tagesfälle

Gesamtausgaben für Tagesfälle

Gesamtausgaben für kurative & rehabilitative Tagesfälle

Gesamtausgaben für Tagesklinik:Langzeitpflege Patienten

Öffentliche Ausgaben für Tagesfälle

Öffentliche Ausgaben für kurative & rehabilitative Tagesfälle

Öffentliche Ausgaben für Tagesklinik: Langzeitpflege Patienten

Private Ausgaben für Tagesfälle

Private Ausgaben für kurative & rehabilitative Tagesfälle

Private Ausgaben für Tagesklinik: Langzeitpflege Patienten

Ausgaben für ambulante Leistungen
Gesamtausgaben für ambulante Leistungen
Gesamtausgaben für ärztliche Leistungen
Gesamtausgaben für zahnärztliche Leistungen
Sonstige Ausgaben für ambulante Leistungen
Öffentliche Ausgaben für ambulante Leistungen
Öffentliche Ausgaben für ärztliche Leistungen
Öffentliche Ausgaben für zahnärztliche Leistungen
Sonstige öffentliche Ausgaben für ambulante Leistungen
Private Ausgaben für ambulante Leistungen

Ausgaben für häusliche Pflege
Gesamtausgaben für häusliche Pflege
Gesamtausgaben für kurative & rehabilitative häusliche Pflege
Gesamtausgaben für häusliche Pflege: Langzeitpflegefälle
Öffentliche Ausgaben für häusliche Pflege
Öffentliche Ausgaben für kurative & rehabilitative häusliche Pflege
Öffentliche Ausgaben für häusliche Pflege: Langzeitpflegefälle
Private Ausgaben für häusliche Pflege
Private Ausgaben für kurative & rehabilitative häusliche Pflege
Private Ausgaben für häusliche Pflege: Langzeitpflegefälle

Ausgaben für sonstige Leistungen
Gesamtausgaben für sonstige Leistungen
Gesamtausgaben für biomedizinische Analysen
Gesamtausgaben Röntgen/Bildgerätetechnik
Gesamtausgaben für Krankentransporte & Rettungsdienste
Andere Gesamtausgaben für sonstige Leistungen
Öffentliche Ausgaben für sonstige Leistungen
Öffentliche Ausgaben für biomedizinische Analysen
Öffentliche Ausgaben Röntgen/Bildgerätetechnik
Öffentliche Ausgaben für Krankentransporte & Rettungsdienste
Andere Öffentliche Ausgaben für sonstige Leistungen
Private Ausgaben für sonstige Leistungen

Ausgaben für medizinische Güter im ambulanten Bereich

Gesamtausgaben für medizinische Güter
Gesamtausgaben für medizinische Güter
Öffentliche Ausgaben für medizinische Güter
Private Ausgaben für medizinische Güter

Arzneimittel und sonstige medizinische Verbrauchsartikel
Gesamtausgaben für Arzneimittel & sonst.med. Verbrauchsartikel
Gesamtausgaben: rezeptpflichtige Arzneimittel
Gesamtausgaben: rezeptfreie Arzneimittel
Sonstige medizinische Verbrauchsartikel
. Öffentliche Ausgaben Arzneimittel & sonst. med. Verbrauchsartikel
Private Ausgaben Arzneimitt. u. sonst. med. Verbrauchsartikel

Therapeutische Hilfsmittel & medizinische Verbrauchsartikel
Gesamtausgaben therapeutische Hilfsmittel & medizinische Verbrauchsartikel
Öffentliche Ausgaben therapeutische Hilfsmittel & medizinische Verbrauchsartikel
Private Ausgaben therapeutische Hilfsmittel & medizinische Verbrauchsartikel

Laufende Gesundheitsausgaben nach Anbieter
Krankenhausleistungen (laufende Gesamtausgaben)
Krankenhausleistungen (laufende öffentliche Ausgaben)
Krankenhausleistungen (laufende private Ausgaben)
Pflegeleistungen & speziellen Pflegeeinrichtungen (LG)
Pflegeleistungen & speziellen Pflegeeinrichtungen (LÖA)
Pflegeleistungen & speziellen Pflegeeinrichtungen (LPA)
Anbieter ambulanter Gesundheitsleistungen (LG)
Anbieter ambulanter Gesundheitsleistungen (LÖA)
Anbieter ambulanter Gesundheitsleistungen (LPA)
Einzelhandel & sonstige Anbieter mediz. Hilfsmittel (LG)

Deutsch

Beschäftigte in der pharmazeutischen Industrie

Lohnkosten der pharmazeutischen Industrie

Arzneimittelverbrauch

Alimentäres System und Stoffwechsel

Antacida

Mitt.bei pept. ulkus & gastroesophagealer re-
fluxkrank.

Antidiabetika

Blut und Blut bildende Organe

Kardiovaskuläres System

Herzglykoside

Antiarrhythmika, Klasse I und III

Antihypertonika

Diuretika

Beta-Adrenorezeptor-Antagonisten

Calciumkanalblocker

Mittel mit Wirkung auf das Renin-Angiotensin-
System

Cholesterin und Triglycerid Senkende Mittel

Sexualhormone & Modulatoren des Genitalsys-
tems

Antiinfektiva zur Systemischen Anwendung

Antibiotika zur Systemischen Anwendung

Muskel- und Skelettsystem

N-steroidale Antiphlogistika und Antirheumatika

Nervensystem

Analgetika

Anxiolytika

Hypnotika und Sedativa

Antidepressiva

Respirationstrakt

Mittel bei Obstruktiven Atemwegserkrankun-
gen

Arzneimittelabsatz

Gesamtinlandsarzneimittelabsatz

A-Alimentäres System und Stoffwechsel

B-Blut und Blut bildende Organe

C-Kardiovaskuläres System

D-Dermatika

G-Urogenitalsystem und Sexualhormone

H-Systemische Hormonpräparate, ex. Sex.hor-
mone/Insuline

J-Antiinfektiva zur Systemischen Anwendung

L-Antineoplastische und immunmodulierende
Mittel

M-Muskel- und Skelettsystem

N-Nervensystem

P-Antiparasitäre Mittel, Insektizide und Repel-
lenzien

R-Respirationstrakt

S-Sinnesorgane

V-Varia

Sonstige Arzneimittel

TEIL 8 - NICHTMEDIZINISCHE GESUNDHEITSFAKTOREN

Lebensgewohnheiten und Umwelt

Ernährung

Kalorienzufuhr insgesamt

Proteinzufuhr insgesamt

Butterverbrauch

Zuckerverbrauch

Verbrauch an Obst und Gemüse

Alkoholkonsum

Alkoholkonsum

Tabakkonsum

Tabakkonsum

Körpergewicht

Bevölkerung mit Übergewicht

Bevölkerung mit Fettleibigkeit

Bevölkerung mit Übergewicht oder Fettleibigkeit

Umwelt: Luftqualität

Schwefeloxidemissionen

Stickstoffoxidemissionen

Kohlenstoffmonoxidemissionen

TEIL 9 - DEMOGRAPHISCHE KENNZIFFERN

Derzeitiger Stand

Gesamtbevölkerung

Weibliche Bevölkerung

Männliche Bevölkerung

Fruchtbarkeitsziffer

Geburtenziffer

Todesfälle

Abhängigkeitsrate

Altersstruktur der Bevölkerung

Gesamtbevölkerung
Bevölkerung 0-14 Jahre
Bevölkerung 0-19 Jahre
Bevölkerung über 15 Jahre
Bevölkerung 15-49 Jahre
Bevölkerung 15-64 Jahre
Bevölkerung 20-64 Jahre
Bevölkerung über 65 Jahre
Bevölkerung 65-69 Jahre
Bevölkerung 70-74 Jahre
Bevölkerung 75-79 Jahre
Bevölkerung über 80 Jahre

Umrechnungskurs

BIP-Kaufkraftparität in US$
Kaufkraftparität, Arzneimittel, in US$
US Dollar-Wechselkurs

Erwerbsbevölkerung

Erwerbsbevölkerung
Erwerbspersonen insgesamt
Zivil Beschäftigte
Abhängig Beschäftigte
Teilzeitarbeit
Arbeitslose

Bildungsniveau

Abschluss ISCED 0/1/2
Abschluss ISCED 3/4
Abschluss ISCED 5B
Abschluss ISCED 5A/6
Erwartete Schulverweildauer
Öffentliche und private Gesamtausgaben für
Bildungseinrichtungen

TEIL 10 - WIRTSCHAFTLICHE KENNZIFFERN

Volkswirtschaftliche Indikatoren

Bruttoinlandsprodukt
Öffentlicher Endverbrauch
Endverbrauch privater Haushalte
Bruttoanlage investitionen
Gesamtausgaben des Staates
Einnahmen des Staates
Bruttolohn- und Gehaltssumme
Durchschnittliches Arbeitereinkommen
Staatsausgaben für F&E (Gesamt)

Deutsch

BIBLIOGRAPHIE

Neueste OECD-Veröffentlichungen im Gesundheitsbereich

HEALTH AT A GLANCE : OECD Indicators 2003 (2003)

SOCIETY AT A GLANCE (2002)
OECD Social indicators, Edition 2002

MEASURING UP: IMPROVING HEALTH SYSTEMS PERFORMANCE IN OECD COUNTRIES (2002)

OECD SOCIAL EXPENDITURE DATABASE, 1980-1998 (2001)
in Englisch und Französisch auf CD-ROM erhältlich

REFORMS FOR AN AGEING SOCIETY (2000)

A SYSTEM OF HEALTH ACCOUNTS (2000)

Health Working Papers:

Eine neue Reihe, ursprünglich für den internen Gebrauch in der OECD erstellter Gesundheitsstudien, die einer breiteren Leserschaft zugänglich gemacht werden sollen, kann unter www.oecd.org/els/ helath/workingpapers kostenlos heruntergeladen werden.

Zu den jüngsten Ausgaben gehören:

Health-Care Systems: Lessons from the Reform Experience (OECD Health Working Papers No.9) December 2003

Private Health Insurance in Australia: A Case Study (OECD Health Working Papers No.8) October 2003

Explaining Waiting Times Variations for Elective Surgery across OECD Countries (OECD Health Working Paper No.7) October 2003

Tackling Excessive Waiting Times for Elective Surgery: A Comparison of Policies in Twelve OECD Countries (OECD Health Working Paper No.6) July 2003

Stroke Care in OECD Countries: A Comparison of Treatment, Costs and Outcomes in 17 Countries (OECD Health Working Papers NO.5) June 2003

Survey of Pharmacoeconomic Assessment Activity in Eleven Countries (OECD Health Working Paper NO.4) May 2003

OECD Study of Cross-National Differences in the Treatment, Costs and Outcomes of Ischaemic Heart Disease (OECD Health Working Paper NO.3) April 2003

Investment in Population Health in Five OECD Countries (OECD Health Working Paper N°2) April 2003

Pharmaceutical Use and Expenditure for Cardiovascular Disease and Stroke: a Study of 12 OECD Countries (OECD Health Working Papers No.1) February 2003

Sonderbeiträge zur Sozialpolitik im Gesundheitsbereich Jüngste Beiträge (Social policyoccasional papers):

Kann unter http://www.oecd.org/findDocument/0,2350,en_2649_33929_1_119684_1_2_1,00.html kostenlos heruntergeladen warden. Die neuesten Freigaben sind:

No. 57 IMPROVING THE PERFORMANCE OF HEALTH CARE SYSTEMS: FROM MEASURES TO ACTION (2001) Zeynep Or

No. 56 AN ASSESSMENT OF THE PERFORMANCE OF THE JAPANESE HEALTH CARESYSTEM (2001) Hyoung-Sun Jeong und Jeremy Hurst

No. 53 TOWARDS MORE CHOICE IN SOCIAL PROTECTION? INDIVIDUAL CHOICE OF INSURER IN BASIC MANDATORY HEALTH INSURANCE IN SWITZERLAND (2001) Francesca Colombo

No. 47 PERFORMANCE MEASUREMENT AND PERFORMANCE MANAGEMENT IN OECD HEALTH SYSTEMS (2001) Jeremy Hurst und Melissa Jee-Hughes

Wegen einer vollständigen Liste wenden Sie sich bitte an den OECD Online Bookshop unter
www.oecd.org/bookshop
oder fordern Sie auf schriftlichem Wege einen Gratiskatalog an bei
OECD Publications Service
2, rue André-Pascal, 75775 PARIS CEDEX16

Deutsch

ECO–SALUD OCDE 2004

ANÁLISIS COMPARATIVO DE 30 PAÍSES

Guía de utilización

Español

ECO-SALUD OCDE 2004 se ha realizado conjuntamente por el Secretariado de la OCDE y el IRDES (Institut de Recherche et d'Etude en Economie de la Santé).

El equipo de *Eco-Salud OCDE 2004* está formado por Gaëlle Balestat, Marie-Clémence Canaud, Manfred Huber, Gaetan Lafortune, David Morgan y Eva Orosz. El equipo del IRDES está formado por Catherine Banchereau, Martine Broïdo, Jacques Harrouin, Christophe Lainé, Florence Naudin y Thierry Rochereau.

Para cualquier problema a cerca de los datos y de las fuentes y métodos, diríjanse a :	**Para cualquier cuestión técnica, diríjanse a :**
Unidad de Políticas Sanitarias OCDE 2, rue André Pascal F-75775 París Cedex 16 (Francia) Fax : (33) 1 44 30 63 61 E-mail : health.contact@oecd.org	**IRDES** 10, rue Vauvenargues F-75018 París (Francia) Fax :(33) 1 53 93 43 50 (pregunten por el equipo Eco-Salud) E-mail : ecosante@irdes.fr Web : www.irdes.fr

Preguntas frecuentemente planteadas

En lo que se refiere a las preguntas tipo que habrán de plantearse en el 2004, la OCDE y el IRDES se esforzarán rápidamente para difundir soluciones, a través de sus direcciones de Internet, así como actualizaciones de los datos, informaciones complementarias sobre las variables, ejemplos de cuadros y la fecha de publicación prevista de *Eco-Salud OCDE 2005*.

● En caso de problemas técnicos, consulte : www.irdes.fr/ecosante/faq.htm
● Para obtener información y actualización de datos, consulte : www.oecd.org/health/healthdata/ (y haga clic en **[Frequently Asked Questions]**) desde la página web de *OECD Health Data*.

Información sobre *Eco-Salud OCDE 2004* en **Internet** :

● www.oecd.org/health/healthdata/
● www.irdes.fr/ecosante/index.htm

El software *Eco-Salud OCDE 2004* está compuesto por :
● un CD-ROM que contiene el programa y los archivos ;
● la presente Guía de utilización.

PREFACIO

Después de más de quince años de recolección de información estadística, la OCDE presenta ahora la décimatercera edición de su base de datos electrónica sobre los sistemas de salud. La edición 2004 incluye nuevos datos en un programa informático que ha sido mejorado. Debido a las aportaciones de los proveedores originales de los datos, estos archivos constituyen una herramienta sumamente rica que esclarece y ayuda a comprender la evolución o el nivel de las series estadísticas. Finalmente, para la versión bajo entorno Windows 98/2000/NT/Me/XP, se han reexaminado las aplicaciones funcionales de *Eco-Salud OCDE* y se han introducido diversas modificaciones de menor cuantía a este software, fácil de usar, que ha dado sendas pruebas de valía y goza de la estima de miles de usuarios.

Se agradece sinceramente el apoyo financiero de los Centers for Medicare and Medicaid Services (CMS, ex HCFA) de los Estados Unidos de América, lo que ha facilitado considerablemente el desarrollo del software. Este programa también debe mucho a los cientos de estadísticos de los 30 países Miembros, que han producido la gran cantidad de datos presentados y la información cualitativa en la que se sustentan.

Español

INTRODUCCIÓN

Eco-Salud OCDE 2004 presenta de forma interactiva y sistemática datos referentes a un gran número de aspectos de los sistemas de salud de los 30 países Miembros de la OCDE, sobre su contexto demográfico, económico y social en general.

La versión 2004 del software *Eco-Salud OCDE* bajo Windows se utiliza de forma muy fácil y rápida, y permite a los utilizadores de un microordenador interrogar los archivos Salud de la OCDE y analizarlos a partir de tablas, gráficos o representaciones cartográficas. *Eco-Salud OCDE* ofrece también opciones de exportación de los datos para su utilización en otros programas. El utilizador selecciona las variables, los países y los años según su opción. La base de datos se compone de, aproximadamente, 1200 series que abarcan el período desde 1960 a 2002. Las series más largas se remontan hasta 1960, si bien la mayoría de los datos se suelen centrar en los años ochenta y noventa. Asímismo, hay muchas series que llegan hasta 2001 ó 2002 y que cubren el año 2003, sobre la base de proyecciones elaboradas por el Secretariado.

Eco-Salud OCDE 2004 se ha presentado en versión plurilingüe (español/francés/inglés/alemán) bajo Windows 98/2000/NT/Me/XP. Este software se ha creado conjuntamente por la OCDE y el IRDES, y es el resultado de la experiencia de ambos organismos en campos de estudio complementarios:

- la publicación y actualización de indicadores estadísticos de salud y sus políticas económicas en los 30 países Miembros de la OCDE ;
- el desarrollo de una base de datos macroeconómica que describe el funcionamiento de un sistema de salud.

Este manual tiene por objeto guiar al utilizador del software por medio de informaciones sobre el contenido de sus bases de datos, las funciones de análisis que ofrece, y sobre su utilización práctica.

Novedades de la versión 2004 de *Eco-Salud OCDE*

La versión 2004 de *Eco-Salud OCDE* contiene un cierto número de mejoras y novedades :

- Nuevo procedimiento de instalación ;
- Aplicación completamente rediseñada siguiendo el estilo Windows-XP ;
- Incorporación en el apartado *Fuentes y Métodos* de un sistema de busqueda por palabras clave o por textos enteros, junto con un nuevo indice de busqueda ;
- Nuevas funciones para imprimir y exportar las *Definiciones, Fuentes y Métodos* ;
- Programa informático y lista de las variables disponibles en ruso ;
- Más opciones para cambiar de idioma (un solo click para obtener todas las funciones en el mismo idioma) ;
- Se incluyen en el hipertexto los resultados preliminares del Proyecto de la OCDE sobre la Salud.

> Las modificaciones o complementos de último minuto introducidos en *Eco-Salud OCDE 2004* se presentan en el archivo **ReadMe.txt**. Este archivo se podrá consultar al finalizar el procedimiento de instalación. Para su lectura ulterior, bastará hacer clic en el icono ReadMe de *Eco-Salud OCDE 2004*.

CAPÍTULO PRIMERO: INSTALACIÓN DE *ECO-SALUD OCDE 2004*

Características mínimas del equipo necesario y configuración del sistema

Para utilizar este software, se necesita :

- Windows 98/2000/NT/Me/XP ;
- 64 MB de RAM ;
- 75 MB de espacio disponible en el disco duro ;
- una unidad de CD-ROM (el CD-ROM se utilizará únicamente durante la fase de instalación del software) ;
- Carta gráfica: 16bits 800x600.

Cuando el disco duro de su ordenador contiene una versión anterior de *Eco-Salud OCDE*, se recomienda suprimirla con objeto de no sobrecargar inútilmente el disco. En el Control Panel (Panel de Controlo), seleccione el icono **[Add/Remove Programs]** (Añadir/Suprimir Programas). Nótese que su listado personal de tablas salvaguardadas no puede ser transferido de una versión de *Eco-Salud* a otra.

Instalación de *Eco-Salud OCDE 2004*

Para dar comienzo al proceso de instalación, inicie Windows e inserte el CD-ROM en el lector. La instalación específica de Eco-Salud OECD en red figura detallada en un recuadro, más adelante, para que pueda ser consultado por el administrador de la red.

Antes de proceder a la instalación del software, se debe cerrar todas las aplicaciones y desactivar el anti-virus de su PC. Verifique asimismo que posee los derechos de instalación de un software en su PC, consultando al administrador de la red o al administrador de su PC.

El CD-ROM se utilizará únicamente durante la fase de instalación del software.

- Haga clic en **[Start]** (Iniciar) y seleccione **[Run]** (Ejecutar) ;
- En el menú **[Open]** (Abrir), teclee **"d:\install"** cuando, por ejemplo, su lector de CD-ROM corresponde a la unidad d (la opción de la unidad será la definida en la configuración de su equipo) ;
- Confirme la selección con **[OK]** ;

Cuando la unidad de CD-ROM está configurada en "AutoBoot", la instalación de *Eco-Salud OCDE 2004* se inicia automáticamente en el momento de la introducción del CD-ROM en el lector.

La instalación se desarrolla en cinco etapas :

- En primer lugar, se solicita al usuario seleccionar el idioma deseado durante la instalación : español, inglés, francés, o alemán ;
- El usuario debe aceptar el contrato Copyright del software ;
- Se debe teclear el **número de serie** del CD-ROM, que se encuentra escrito en el **reverso de la portada**

de esta **Guía de utilización**. Si este número es correcto, el procedimiento de instalación prosigue. En caso contrario, aparece un mensaje de error y se debe volver a introducir el número de serie ;

- A continuación, el usuario debe elegir el directorio en el que desea instalar el software. El programa efectúa una verificación del espacio disponible. Cuando no se dispone de espacio suficiente en el disco, el usuario debe entonces liberar espacio en el disco o cambiar el directorio de destino ;

- La ultima ventana invita al usuario a confirmar sus selecciones. La instalación de los archivos del sistema prosigue automáticamente.

Al finalizar la instalación, se habrá creado un repertorio que contiene los iconos necesarios para utilizar *Eco-Salud OCDE 2004*.

A continuación aparece una ventana con los contactos útiles en caso de tener dudas sobre el software, así como las direcciones de Internet de la OCDE y del IRDES.

Nota: es posible que el usuario tenga que apagar el ordenador tras el proceso de instalación, lo cual, de darse el caso, le sería advertido por el programa.

Carácter específico de la instalación de *Eco-Salud OCDE 2004* en red

Para que el programa esté en red, el administrador debe instalarlo en una unidad de la red accesible a todos los usuarios potenciales. Esta fase es similar a la instalación standard (mencionada anteriormente).

A continuación, el administrador de la red debe instalar el subdirectorio "Client" en cada terminal de trabajo. Para ello, deberá lanzar el programa **Install.exe**, que se encuentra en el repertorio **USER**.

Por ejemplo, si el software se ha instalado en el directorio E:\APPLI\ECOSANTE2004, se deberá ir a : E:\APPLI\ECOSANTE2004\USER\INSTALL.EXE.

El programa de instalación del subdirectorio "Client" hace que se cree automáticamente el directorio C:\ecowin2004. Si se desea mover el repertorio local del usuario, se deberán modificar los parámetros LocalPath del archivo Ecowin.ini que se encuentra en el repertorio Windows.

Los trabajos salvaguardados por los usuarios se sitúan por defecto en el directorio local C:\ecowin2004\ result. Gracias a ello, cada usuario puede guardar y disponer de sus propios grupos de países y tablas salvaguardadas. El subdirectorio "Cliente" ocupa menos de I MB del disco duro del usuario.

Inicio de *Eco-Salud OCDE 2004*

Seleccione [**Start-up - Programmes - OECD Health Data 2004**] (Iniciar-Programas), y posiciónese en [**OECD Health Data**].

Para permitir un correcto funcionamiento del software, es importante que el disco duro disponga por lo menos de 5 MB tras la instalación, con objeto de almacenar los archivos de trabajo y de salvaguardia.

Una vez iniciado el programa, se pueden someter a prueba las distintas opciones dejándose guiar por los menús sucesivos y refiriéndose a las zonas de información de las ventanas.

Las Info-burbujas - véase más adelante - están automáticamente activadas durante la primera utilización del software. No obstante, se aconseja leer este manual para saber más sobre la utilización práctica del software.

Desinstalación del programa

Para desinstalar *Eco-Salud OCDE 2004*, salga del programa.

Haga clic en el menú [Start-up], seleccione Settings (Propriedades). En el Control Panel (Panel de Control), seleccione el icono [Add/Remove Programs] (Añadir/Suprimir Programas). Seleccione [Eco-Salud OCDE 2004] en la lista y haga clic en [Add/Remove Programs] (Añadir/Suprimir). Haga clic en [OK] para confirmar la desinstalación del programa.

Este programa suprime todos los archivos de *Eco-Salud OCDE 2004*. Para desinstalar el programa, no necesita utilizar el CD-ROM.

Actualización de los datos a través de Internet

Es posible que se detecten errores en las series estadísticas, o bien que se hayan actualizado o añadido datos suplementarios después de la publicación de *Eco-Salud OCDE 2004*. Se recomienda por eso integrar estos nuevos valores en su software a través de una de las dos direcciones de Internet mencionadas a continuación

En Internet :

- conéctese a una de las direcciones siguientes :
  - ⇨ la dirección de la OCDE: www.oecd.org/health/healthdata ;
  - ⇨ la dirección del IRDES: www.irdes.fr/ecosante/index.htm ;
- clique en **[Updates]** desde la dirección de Internet de la OCDE, o bien en **[Mise à jour des données]** desde la dirección de Internet del IRDES ;
- clique dos veces en **[Download]** (**[Chargement]**) e indique el repertorio del microordenador en el cual se desean copiar los archivos cargados.

En Windows :

- Una vez cargado el archivo clique dos veces en el ícono o la palabra para iniciar la instalación.
- El archivo cargado constituye un archivo comprimido auto-extractible (.EXE) que contiene a su vez 2 archivos :
  - ⇨ la actualización de la base de datos propiamente dicha ;
  - ⇨ un archivo Leame que explica estas actualizaciones ;
- Indique el repertorio en el cual se ha instalado la base de datos *Eco-Salud OCDE 2004* (por ejemplo c:\software\ecowin2004), y clique OK para confirmar;
- Cuando aparezca una ventana con el título de la base de datos y su versión (por ejemplo *Eco-Salud OCDE 2004*. 2nda. ed.) : clique " Start update " para iniciar la actualización.
- En caso de que la actualización no inicie, verifique el repertorio en el cual se ha instalado la base de datos y escriba su nombre de nuevo.

En la ventana principal de *Eco-Salud OCDE 2004*:

Una vez actualizada la base de datos, cambiarán automáticamente la fecha y el nombre de la versión que aparecen bajo el título "*ECO-SALUD OCDE 2004*".

Español

CAPÍTULO SEGUNDO: INTERROGACIÓN DE LA BASE DE DATOS

Descripción de la ventana principal de *Eco-Salud OCDE 2004*

Las diferentes funciones del software se seleccionan por medio de iconos. Un simple clic en uno de estos iconos permite, bien efectuar la acción inherente a la función deseada, bien obtener una pantalla que posibilita la realización de esta función tras haber seleccionado los distintos parámetros.

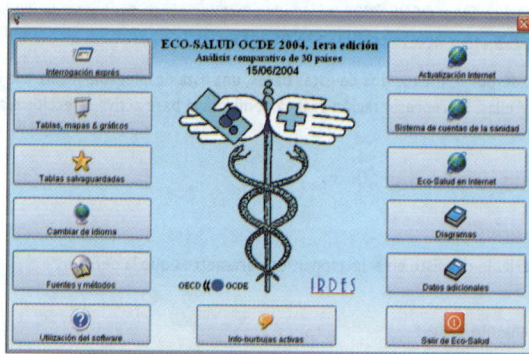

[Interrogación exprés] permite seleccionar una variable para obtener los valores de un país o de todos los países, para uno, dos o todos los años disponibles y, asimismo, calcular las tasas de crecimiento para el período correspondiente. Esta función permite también la construcción de mapas y la impresión o la exportación de una tabla realizada.	**[Fuentes y métodos]** permite acceder al contenido de la ayuda para la utilización de las variables, es decir, a las definiciones y a las fuentes y métodos correspondientes. **[Salir de Eco-Salud]** termina la sesión.
[Tablas, mapas y gráficos] permite seleccionar una o varias variables para obtener los valores de uno o varios países, para uno o más años, y calcular las tasas de crecimiento para el período correspondiente. Esta función permite también construir mapas y gráficos.	**[Utilización del software]** permite acceder al contenido de la ayuda a cerca del software.
[Tablas salvaguardadas] permite seleccionar una tabla previamente guardada por el usuario o predefinida por la Unidad de Políticas de Salud. Así, esta función permite al usuario crear su propia lista de tablas.	**[Info-burbujas]** activa o desactiva la visualización de la información que aparece sobre los iconos y las distintas funciones del software.
[Cambiar de idioma] permite seleccionar un idioma de trabajo para el software (alemán, español, francés o inglés) y un idioma para la ayuda (inglés o francés).	**[Acceso directo a Internet]** : los iconos que contienen este logotipo permiten el acceso directo a direcciones de Internet OECD relacionadas con la Salud, incluyendo la dirección para actualizar los datos a través de Internet.

Español

Ayudas

Ayuda sobre la utilización de las variables : Fuentes y Métodos

Esta función es accesible de diferentes modos: de forma contextual, o a partir de un índice general.

Para obtener la ayuda contextual, haga clic en el botón derecho del ratón, posicionándose a nivel del elemento sobre el que se desea obtener la definición standard, la fuente y/o las diferencias conocidas con respecto a la definición standard. En *Eco-Salud OCDE 2004* se accede a esta ayuda tanto desde la lista de capítulos como desde la de variables.

Para acceder al índice general de ayuda a la utilización de las variables (Fuentes y Métodos), haga clic en el icono **[Fuentes]** cuando esté disponible. Seleccione el capítulo, y a continuación la variable sobre la que desea obtener la información.

Además del programa *Eco-Salud OCDE 2004*, se pueden instalar otras dos bases de datos, difundidas por el IRDES: Eco-Salud FRANCIA y Eco-Salud REGIONAL (Francia).

Cuando se han instalado por lo menos dos de estas bases, una lista desplegable frente a la base activa permite la selección de una de ellas. La representación gráfica confirma la base activa seleccionada.

Creación de tablas, mapas y gráficos

Selección de las variables

La elección de una variable consiste en seleccionar los parámetros que la definen :

- el **capítulo** ;
- la **variable** propiamente dicha ;
- la **unidad** que se trata de asociar.

Para acceder a la lista de las variables, haga clic en el botón **[Añadir]** de la viñeta **"Variables"** o en la zona vacía del selector.

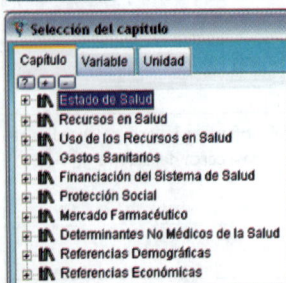

⇨ Los títulos de los capítulos, variables y unidades aparecen en la pantalla de forma abreviada, pero suficientemente explícita.

⇨ Su encadenamiento lógico permite elegir sin dificultad le secuencia que desemboca en la variable deseada. En el Capítulo 3 de esta Guía, se presenta un listado de las variables.

En el selector de **"capítulo"**, se encuentran disponibles tres botones :

Un clic en el botón **[+]** presenta, para el conjunto de los capítulos de un mismo nivel, el detalle del nivel inferior (el clic sobre el botón **[+]** puede intervenir para los distintos niveles : para obtener todos los capítulos "padres" contenidos en los capítulos "abuelos" y, acto seguido, en todos los capítulos "hijos" contenidos en los capítulos "padres"). Inversamente, un clic en el botón **[-]** de este selector, reduce el detalle propuesto al nivel inferior. Un clic en **[?]** permite acceder a la ayuda sobre el software.

Selección múltiple

Existe otra forma de seleccionar variables comunes a varios capítulos, aunque para ello se requiere conocerpreviamente el contenido de los capítulos en cuestión. Para ello, haga clic en la opción **[Multiselección]**.

Unas casillas aparecen delante del nombre de los capítulos: haga clic en las correspondientes a los capítulos que contienen las variables deseadas.

Una vez elegidos, haga clic en la flecha **[Siguiente]**. Así aparecerá la ventana de selección de las variables presentando únicamente las variables comunes a los capítulos previamente seleccionados. Para seleccionar la(s) variable(s) y la(s) unidad(es), siga el mismo procedimiento.

Selección de los países

Para acceder a la selección de los países, haga clic en la viñeta **"Países"**.

La lista de países de la OCDE se encuentra situada en la parte superior izquierda de la ventana; los grupos de países se hallan en la parte inferior de esta ventana; a la derecha se pueden encontrar los países o grupos de países que se hayan seleccionado.

Selección de un país (o de varios)

Para seleccionar un país :

- bien, haga doble clic en el país deseado ;
- o bien, haga un único clic en el país y, acto seguido, haga clic en el botón **[+]**.

Para seleccionar todos los países, haga clic en el botón **[++]**. Todos los países aparecen entonces en la ventana de la derecha.

Diagramas de los Sistemas de Salud

La ayuda relativa a los sistemas de salud de los países es accesible, bien de forma contextual, o bien por medio de un índice general. Esta ayuda incluye, para la mayor parte de los países de la OCDE, diagramas descriptivos de los actores que intervienen en el "mercado" de la asistencia sanitaria y sus interrelaciones.

En ciertos casos, se presentan dos o varios gráficos para un mismo país, mostrando así la evolución de las reformas que han tenido lugar en ese país durante la última década o incluso anteriormente.

Se puede acceder a la ayuda contextual haciendo clic con el botón derecho del ratón sobre el país para el cual se desea obtener la ayuda.

Para acceder al índice general de los sistemas, haga clic en el botón **[Sistema]**. Seleccione el país sobre el cual se desea obtener dicha información.

Selección de los años y períodos

Para calcular las tasas de crecimiento se requiere la selección previa de años y períodos, haciendo clic en la viñeta **"Años y Períodos"**.

La columna de la izquierda presenta los años para los que se dispone de cifras. Dado que no se dispone de datos para todas las variables y países, se puede consultar su disponibilidad, haciendo clic en el botón **[Disponibilidad]**, en la parte baja derecha de la ventana.

Botones azules = años para los cuales se encuentran disponibles las cifras
Botones verdes = años seleccionados

Visualización de una tabla

Antes de poder visualizar una tabla, aparece una ventana aconsejando la prudencia en la comparación de los datos entre diferentes países.

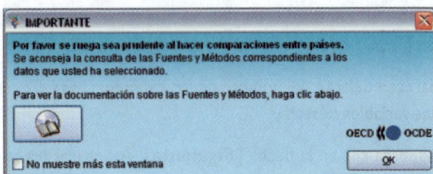

Haga clic en **[OK]** para visualizar los datos.

Barra de herramientas de las tablas

La barra de herramientas contiene los iconos cuyas funciones son las siguientes :

Reduce / aumenta la dimensión de la barra de herramientas.

100% ▼ Reduce / aumenta la dimensión de la hoja activa.

Ajusta la anchura de todas la columnas de forma automática (la anchura de cada columna se determina en función de su contenido).

Permite fijar la misma anchura para todas las columnas de la tabla tomando como referencia la columna activa.

Activa / desactiva la cuadrícula.

Activa/desactiva la ventana con leyendas.

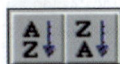

Clasifica los elementos de la tabla por orden creciente o decreciente de los datos contenidos en la columna activa.

Añade una columna y precisa su posición y contenido.

Suprime la columna de la tabla de la que se precise la posición (por defecto, la posición indicada corresponde a la de la columna activa).

Permite calcular un indicio comparativo.

Permite añadir una columna para clasificar los resultados.

Permite obtener la media aritmética de los valores de la columna activa (el resultado aparece en la última línea).

Permite obtener la suma de los valores de la columna activa (el resultado aparece en la última línea).

Abre la ventana de configuración de la impresión de las tablas.

Abre la ventana de exportación de las tablas.

Permite copiar la zona activa en el portapapeles y pegar su contenido en otra aplicación Windows (opción **[Pegar]** del menú Edición o el comando **[Ctrl+V]**).

Permite acceder al módulo de construcción de gráficos.

Permite construir un mapa a partir de la columna seleccionada, cuando las filas de la tabla corresponden a países.

Permite acceder a la ayuda sobre la utilización del software.

Permite acceder a la ayuda sobre las variables (Fuentes y Métodos).

Permite salir de la ventana de visualización de la tabla.

Para modificar el título de las columnas, haga doble clic en estas últimas. Para modificar el título de la tabla, haga doble clic en la celda vacía en la parte superior izquierda de la tabla.

Se puede acceder a las funciones de la barra de herramientas haciendo clic con el botón de la derecha del ratón en el título de una de las columnas de una tabla. Haciendo clic con el botón de la derecha del ratón en el título de una variable (si las variables están en una fila y los años o los países en una columna) mostrará directamente la definición, fuente y método del indicador seleccionado.

Exportación de la tabla

La configuración de la exportación es accesible a partir de la barra de herramientas, tras haber entrado en la ventana **"Ver la tabla"**.

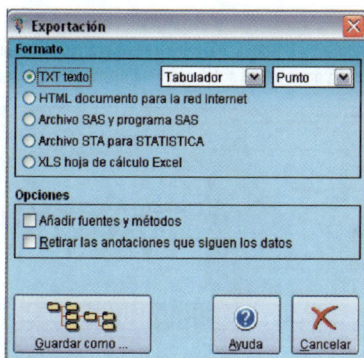

Se proponen cinco tipos de exportación :

- ## Texto .TXT

Esta opción permite obtener un archivo de tipo texto fácilmente utilizable, pudiéndose elegir el separador de columnas (tabulador, espacio, coma, punto y coma), y el separador de decimales (punto o coma).

- ## Sistema SAS

El sistema SAS requiere dos archivos: el primero, que contiene los datos (extensión "DAT"), y el segundo, que incluye la descripción de las variables y la subdivisión del archivo de datos (extensión "SAS"). Para importar este archivo en el software SAS, es preciso ejecutar el programa. Este último genera, a partir del archivo de datos, un archivo en el directorio provisional de SAS (Work), cuyo resultado puede ser consultado en el entorno SAS (para más información sobre SAS: www.sas.com/).

Haga clic en el botón **[Guardar como]** para elegir el camino de salvaguardia. Aparece entonces una nueva ventana que indica por defecto el directorio en el cual se está trabajando. Según los procedimientos propios de Windows, el usuario puede dirigirse hacia los distintos directorios y elegir aquel en que desea colocar sus archivos. Atribuya un nombre al archivo en la línea Archivo de esta ventana. Por defecto, la extensión es aquella que corresponde al formato de exportación seleccionado. Haga clic en el botón **[Save]** (Guardar). Un mensaje "Archivo salvaguardado" indica que la exportación del archivo se ha desarrollado correctamente. Haga clic en **[Cancelar]** para volver de nuevo a la ventana **"Exportación"**.

- ## Archivo STA para STATISTICA

Este formato permite crear un archivo de extensión .STA para el programa estadístico Statistica, de la compañía StatSoft (www.statsoft.com/). En el archivo aparecen el título de la tabla, los datos y las etiquetas de las variables.

- ## HTML

Este formato permite crear una tabla que puede visualizarse mediante un buscador de Internet como Netscape o Internet Explorer. La ventaja de este tipo de documentos es que pueden visualizarse directamente con la mayoría de ordenadores (PC, Macintosh, Station Unix, etc.).

- ## Excel .XLS

Esta opción permite recuperar directamente los datos en Excel, versión 4.0 ó superior, sin tener que cambiar su formato. Los títulos de la tabla exportada aparecen en una celda de la hoja de cálculo Excel en la parte superior izquierda de la tabla. (Para más información sobre Excel: http://office.microsoft.com/home/default.aspx).

Módulo gráfico

El módulo gráfico ha sido mejorado y ahora permite crear gráficos complejos, con la selección de datos directamente desde la tabla. La ayuda sobre el software está disponible desde el botón "Ayuda" en el gráfico.

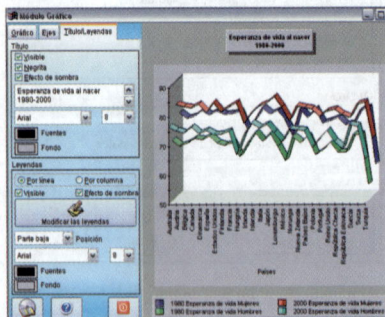

CAPÍTULO TERCERO: LISTA DE VARIABLES DE LA EDICIÓN 2004

PARTE I - ESTADO DE SALUD

Mortalidad

Esperanza de vida
Mujeres al nacer
Mujeres de 40 años
Mujeres de 60 años
Mujeres de 65 años
Mujeres de 80 años
Hombres al nacer
Hombres de 40 años
Hombres de 60 años
Hombres de 65 años
Hombres de 80 años
Mujeres y hombres al nacer

Causas de mortalidad
Todas las causas
Enfermedades infecciosas y parasitarias
Enfermedades por VIH
Tumores malignos
Tumores malignos del colon
Tumores malignos de pulmón
Tumores malignos de mama (mujeres)
Tumores malignos del cuello del útero
Tumores malignos de próstata
Enfermedades de la sangre
Enfermedades endócrinas, alimenticias y del metabolismo
Diabetes mellitus
Trastornos mentales y de comportamiento
Enfermedades del sistema nervioso
Enfermedades del sistema circulatorio
Enfermedades isquémicas del corazón
Infarto agudo de miocardio
Enfermedades cerebrovasculares
Enfermedades del sistema respiratorio
Neumonía y gripe
Bronquitis, asma y enfisema
Enfermedades del sistema digestivo
Enfermedades crónicas del hígado y cirrosis
Enfermedades de la piel y tejido subcutáneo

Enfermedades del sistema osteomuscular
Enfermedades de los órganos genitourinarios
Embarazo, parto y post-parto
Condiciones perinatales
Anomalías congénitas
Síntomas y estados morbosos mal definidos
Causas externas
Accidentes automovilísticos
Caídas accidentales
Lesiones intencionales
Agresiones
Efectos adversos de medicamentos
Complicaciones médicas

Mortalidad infantil y materna
Mortalidad infantil
Mortalidad neonatal
Mortalidad perinatal
Mortalidad materna

Disminución de la esperanza de vida
Todas las causas
Enfermedades infecciosas y parasitarias
Enfermedades por VIH
Tumores malignos
Tumores malignos del colon
Tumores malignos de pulmón
Tumores malignos de mama (mujeres)
Tumores malignos del cuello del útero
Tumores malignos de próstata
Enfermedades de la sangre
Enfermedades endócrinas, alimenticias y del metabolismo
Diabetes mellitus
Trastornos mentales y de comportamiento
Enfermedades del sistema nervioso
Enfermedades del sistema circulatorio
Enfermedades isquémicas del corazón
Infarto agudo de miocardio
Enfermedades cerebrovasculares
Enfermedades del sistema respiratorio
Neumonía y gripe
Bronquitis, asma y enfisema
Enfermedades del sistema digestivo

Enfermedades crónicas del hígado y cirrosis
Enfermedades de la piel y tejido subcutáneo
Enfermedades del sistema osteomuscular
Enfermedades de los órganos genitourinarios
Embarazo, parto y post-parto
Condiciones perinatales
Anomalías congénitas
Síntomas y estados morbosos mal definidos
Causas externas
Accidentes automovilísticos
Caídas accidentales
Lesiones intencionales
Agresiones
Efectos adversos de medicamentos
Complicaciones médicas

Morbilidad

Percepción del estado de salud
Salud ≥ buena, mujeres, 15-24
Salud ≥ buena, mujeres, 25-44
Salud ≥ buena, mujeres, 45-64
Salud ≥ buena, mujeres, 65+
Salud ≥ buena, mujeres, todas las edades
Salud ≥ buena, hombres, 15-24
Salud ≥ buena, hombres, 25-44
Salud ≥ buena, hombres, 45-64
Salud ≥ buena, hombres, 65+
Salud ≥ buena, hombres, todas las edades
Salud ≥ buena, total, 15-24
Salud ≥ buena, total, 25-44
Salud ≥ buena, total, 45-64
Salud ≥ buena, total, 65+
Salud ≥ buena, población total, todas las edades

Salud infantil
Bajo peso al nacer

Anomalías congénitas
Espina bífida
Transposición de los grandes vasos
Reducción/anomalía de los miembros
Síndrome de Down/Trisomía 21

Salud dental
Dientes cariados/perdidos/obturados

Enfermedades transmisibles
Síndrome de inmunodeficiencia adquirida (SIDA)

Cancer
Tumores malignos

Tumores malignos del colon
Tumores malignos del pulmón
Tumores malignos de mama, mujeres
Tumores malignos del cuello del útero
Tumores malignos de próstata

Accidentes
Heridas por accidentes de tráfico

Absentismo laboral por enfermedad
Ausentismo laboral auto-declarado por enfermedad
Ausentismo laboral compensado por enfermedad

PARTE 2 - RECURSOS EN SALUD

Empleo en salud
Empleo total en salud
Empleo total en hospitales
Médicos en activo
Mujeres médicos en activo
Médicos generalistas en activo
Especialistas en activo
Odontólogos en activo
Farmacéuticos en activo
Personal de enfermería en activo

Camas hospitalarias
Camas hospitalarias de cuidados intensivos
Camas hospitalarias de larga estancia

Relación camas-empleo
Proporción de personal hospitalario en cuidados intensivos
Proporción personal de enfermería en cuidados intensivos

Tecnología médica
Tomografía computada
Imágenes de resonancia magnética
Equipo de radioterapia
Litotritores
Estaciones de hemodiálisis
Mamógrafos

Formación en profesiones de la salud
Titulados médicos, ISCED 3
Titulados médicos, ISCED 4

Titulados médicos, ISCED 5A
Titulados médicos, ISCED 5B
Titulados médicos, ISCED 6

PART 3 - USO DE LOS RECURSOS EN SALUD

Prevención (Vacunación)

Vacunación: Difteria, Tétanos, Tosferina
Vacunación: Sarampión
Vacunación: Gripe

Consultas

Consultas médicas
Consultas odontológicas

Uso de recursos hospitalarios

Jornadas de cuidados intensivos
Tasa de ocupación de camas, hospitales de cuidados intensivos
Tasa de rotación de camas en cuidados intensivos

Duración media de estancia

Duración media de estancia: hospitales, cuidados intensivos

Promedio de estancia en hospitalización
Promedio de estancia en cuidados intensivos

Duración media de estancia, categorías de diagnóstico

Todas las causas
Enfermedades infecciosas y parasitarias
Enfermedades por VIH
Tumores malignos
Tumores malignos del colon
Tumores malignos del pulmón
Tumores malignos de mama, mujeres
Tumores malignos de próstata
Enfermedades de la sangre
Enfermedades endócrinas, alimenticias y del metabolismo
Diabetes mellitus
Enfermedades del sistema nervioso
Catarata senil
Otitis media
Enfermedades del sistema circulatorio
Enfermedades isquémicas del corazón

Infarto agudo de miocardio
Enfermedades cerebrovasculares
Enfermedades del sistema respiratorio
Neumonía y gripe
Bronquitis, asma y enfisema
Enfermedades del sistema digestivo
Ulceras
Apendicitis
Hernia inguinal y femoral
Enfermedades crónicas del hígado y cirrosis
Colelitiasis
Enfermedades de la piel y tejido subcutáneo
Enfermedades del sistema osteomuscular
Osteoartrosis
Complicaciones discosintervertebrales
Osteoporosis
Enfermedades de los órganos genitourinarios
Embarazo, parto y post-parto
Parto normal
Condiciones perinatales
Anomalías congénitas
Síntomas y estados morbosos mal definidos
Causas externas
Fractura del cuello del fémur
Otras categorías no especificadas

Ratio de recurrencia

Ratio de recurrencia por categorías de diagnóstico

Todas las causas
Enfermedades infecciosas y parasitarias
Enfermedades por VIH
Tumores malignos
Tumores malignos del colon
Tumores malignos del pulmón
Tumores malignos de mama, mujeres
Tumores malignos de próstata
Enfermedades de la sangre
Enfermedades endócrinas, alimenticias y del metabolismo
Diabetes mellitus
Enfermedades del sistema nervioso
Catarata senil
Otitis media
Enfermedades del sistema circulatorio
Enfermedades isquémicas del corazón
Infarto agudo de miocardio
Enfermedades cerebrovasculares

Español

Enfermedades del sistema respiratorio
Neumonía y gripe
Bronquitis, asma y enfisema
Enfermedades del sistema digestivo
Ulceras
Apendicitis
Hernia inguinal y femoral
Enfermedades crónicas del hígado y cirrosis
Colelitiasis
Enfermedades de la piel y tejido subcutáneo
Enfermedades del sistema osteomuscular
Osteoartrosis
Complicaciones discosintervertebrales
Osteoporosis
Enfermedades de los órganos genitourinarios
Embarazo, parto y post-parto
Parto normal
Condiciones perinatales
Anomalías congénitas
Síntomas y estados morbosos mal definidos
Causas externas
Fractura del cuello del fémur
Otras categorías no especificadas

Intervenciones quirúrgicas

Total de intervenciones quirúrgicas
Casos quirúrgicos totales (hospitalización + casos diarios)
Casos quirúrgicos totales con hospitalizacíon
Total de casos diarios quirúrgicos

Intervenciones quirúrgicas por ICD-CM
Operación de cataratas
Amigdalectomía con o sin adenoidectomía
Intervenciones coronarias percutáneas
Stenting coronario
Injerto aortocoronario
Cateterización del corazón
Pacemakers (estimulador cardiaco)
Ligación/quitación, venas varicosas
Apendectomía
Colecistectomía
Colecistectomía laparoscópica
Hernia inguinal y femoral
Prostatectomía (transuretal)
Prostatectomía (excepto transuretal)
Histerectomía (sólo vaginal)
Cesárea

Prótesis de la cadera
Prótesis de la rodilla
Cirugía conservativa de mama
Mastectomía

Trasplantes y diálises
Trasplantes de médula ósea
Trasplantes de corazón
Trasplantes de hígado
Trasplantes de pulmón
Trasplantes de riñón
Transplante de riñón funcional
Pacientes con insuficiencia renal
Pacientes dializados
Diálisis a domicilio

PARTE 4 - GASTOS SANITARIOS

Gasto nacional en salud

Gasto total en salud
Gasto total en salud
Gasto corriente total en salud
Inversión total en establecimientos médicos
Gasto público en salud
Gasto corriente público en salud
Inversión pública en establecimientos médicos
Gasto privado en salud
Gasto corriente privado en salud
Inversión privada en establecimientos médicos

Gasto en servicios personales de salud
Gasto total en servicios personales de salud
Gasto público en servicios personales de salud
Gasto privado en servicios personales de salud

Gasto en servicios colectivos de salud
Gasto total en servicios colectivos de salud
Gasto publico en servicios colectivos de salud
Gasto privado en servicios colectivos de salud

Prevención y salud pública
Gasto total en prevención y salud pública
Gasto público en prevención y salud pública
Gasto privado en prevención y salud pública

Gasto en administración y seguros de salud
Gasto total en administración y seguros de salud
Gasto público en administración y seguros de salud

Gasto privado en administración y seguros de salud

Gasto relacionado con la salud
Gasto en formación del personal sanitario
Gasto total en salud I+D
Gasto público en salud I+D

Gasto en atención médica

Gasto en atención médica por funciones
Gasto total en atención médica
Gasto total asistencia curativa y rehabilitación
Gasto total en atención de larga duración
Gasto total en servicios auxiliares
Gasto total en servicios no clasificados por funciones
Gasto público en atención médica
Gasto público asistencia curativa y rehabilitación
Gasto público en atención de larga duración
Gasto público en servicios auxiliares
Gasto público en servicios no clasificados por funciones
Gasto privado en atención médica
Gasto privado asistencia curativa y rehabilitación
Gasto privado en atención de larga duración
Gasto privado en servicios auxiliares
Gasto privado en servicios no clasificados por funciones

Gasto en atención hospitalaria
Gasto total en atención hospitalaria
Gasto total asistencia curativa y rehabilitación hospitalaria
Gasto total en atención de larga duración hospitalaria
Gasto público en atención hospitalaria
Gasto público asistencia curativa y rehabilitación hospitalaria
Gasto público atención de larga duración hospitalaria
Gasto privado en atención hospitalaria
Gasto privado asistencia curativa y rehabilitación hospitalaria
Gasto privado atención de larga duración hospitalaria

Gasto de atención en hospitalización de día
Gasto total en hospitalización de día
Gasto total asistencia curativa y rehabilitación hospitalización de día

Gasto total atención de larga duración hospitalización de día
Gasto público en hospitalización de día
Gasto público asistencia curativa y rehabilitación hospitalización de día
Gasto público atención de larga duración hospitalización de día
Gasto privado en hospitalización de día
Gasto privado asistencia curativa y rehabilitación hospitalización de día
Gasto privado atención de larga duración hospitalización de día

Gasto en atención ambulatoria
Gasto total en atención ambulatoria
Gasto total en servicios médicos
Gasto total en servicios dentales
Otros gastos totales en atención ambulatoria
Gasto público en atención ambulatoria
Gasto público en servicios médicos
Gasto público en servicios dentales
Otros gastos públicos en atención ambulatoria
Gasto privado en atención ambulatoria

Gasto en atención domiciliaria
Gasto total en atención domiciliaria
Gasto total asistencia curativa y rehabilitación domiciliaria
Gasto total atención de larga duración domiciliaria
Gasto público en atención domiciliaria
Gasto público asistencia curativa y rehabilitación domiciliaria
Gasto público atención de larga duración domiciliaria
Gasto privado en atención domiciliaria
Gasto privado asistencia curativa y rehabilitación domiciliaria
Gasto privado atención de larga duración domiciliaria

Gasto en servicios auxiliares
Gasto total en servicios auxiliares
Gasto total en análisis de laboratorios
Gasto total en diagnóstico por imagen
Gasto total en transporte de pacientes y rescate de emergencia
Otros gastos totales en servicios auxiliares
Gasto público en servicios auxiliares
Gasto público en análisis de laboratorios

Español

Gasto público en diagnóstico por imagen

Gasto público en transporte de pacientes y rescate de emergencia

Otros gastos públicos en servicios auxiliares

Gasto privado en servicios auxiliares

Bienes médico-sanitarios para pacientes externos

Gasto total en bienes médicos

Gasto total en bienes médicos

Gasto público en bienes médicos

Gasto privado en bienes médicos

Productos farmacéuticos y otros productos médicos perecederos

Gasto total en productos farmacéuticos

Gastro total en medicinas recetadas

Gasto total en medicinas sin prescripción médica

Otros productos farmacéuticos perecederos

Gasto público en productos farmacéuticos

Gasto privado en productos farmacéuticos

Aparatos terapéuticos y otros productos duraderos

Gasto total en aparatos terapéuticos

Gasto público en aparatos terapéuticos

Gasto privado en aparatos terapéuticos

Gasto corriente en salud por proveedores

Servicios de hospitales (corriente total)

Servicios de hospitales (corriente público)

Servicios de hospitales (corriente privado)

Establecimientos de atención medicalizada y residencial (corriente total)

Establecimientos de atención medicalizada y residencial (corriente público)

Establecimientos de atención medicalizada y residencial (corriente privado)

Proveedores de atencion ambulatoria (corriente total)

Proveedores de atención ambulatoria (corriente público)

Proveedores de atención ambulatoria (corriente privado)

Minoristas y otros proveedores de productos médicos (corriente total)

Minoristas y otros proveedores de productos médicos (corriente público)

Minoristas y otros proveedores de productos médicos (corriente privado)

Suministro y administración de salud pública (corriente total)

Suministro y administración de salud pública (corriente público)

Suministro y administración de salud pública (corriente privado)

Administración de la salud y seguros médicos (corriente total)

Administración de la salud y seguros médicos (corriente público)

Administración de la salud y seguros médicos (corriente privado)

Servicios médicos de otras industrias (corriente total)

Servicios médicos de otras industrias (corriente público)

Servicios médicos de otras industrias (corriente privado)

Gasto por edad y género

Mujeres 65+ / Mujeres 0-64

Mujeres 75+ / Mujeres 0-64

Mujeres 65-74 / Mujeres 0-64

Hombres 65+ / Hombres 0-64

Hombres 75+ / Hombres 0-64

Hombres 65-74 / Hombres 0-64

Población 65+ / Población 0-64

Población 75+ / Población 0-64

Población 65-74 / Población 0-64

Gasto: Población (total)

Gasto: población 0-64 años

Gasto: población 65 años y más

Gasto: población 65-74 años

Gasto: población 75 años y más

Indice de precios

Gasto total en salud

Gasto total en productos farmacéuticos

Gasto público en salud

Consumo privado en salud

PARTE 5 - FINANCIACIÓN DEL SISTEMA DE SALUD

Gasto en salud por fuentes de financiación

Gasto público en salud
Gobierno general, excepto fondos de seguridad social
Sistemas de seguridad social
Gasto privado en salud
Gastos netos de los hogares
Seguros privados
Seguros privados (excluído el seguro social)
Seguros sociales privados
Otras fuentes privadas financiación (incluído resto del mundo)

PARTE 6 - PROTECCIÓN SOCIAL

Gasto social

Gasto total en seguridad social
Ancianidad
Supervivientes
Prestaciones relacionadas con incapacidad
Salud
Familias
Programas de mercado laboral activo
Desempleo
Viviendas
Otros campos de política social

Cobertura sanitaria

Sistema integral de salud
Cuidados intensivos hospitalarios
Atención médica ambulatoria
Productos farmacéuticos

PARTE 7 - MERCADO FARMACÉUTICO

Actividades de la industria farmacéutica

Producción: industria farmacéutica
Valor farmacéutico añadido
Formación bruta de capital de la industria farmacéutica
Exportaciones de la industria farmacéutica (fabricación)
Importaciones de la industria farmacéutica (fabricación)
Gasto en la industria farmacéutica I+D
Asalariados en la industria farmacéutica
Remuneración en la industria farmacéutica
Costos laborales en mayoristas farmacéuticos
Costos laborales en minoristas farmacéuticos

Consumo de medicamentos

Tracto Alimentario y Metabolismo
Antiácidos
Agentes contra la úlcera péptica y el reflujo
Drogas usadas en diabetes
Sangre y Órganos Formadores de Sangre
Sistema Cardiovascular
Glucósidos cardíacos
Antiarrítmicos de Clase I y III
Antihipertensivos
Diuréticos
Agentes beta-bloqueantes
Bloqueantes de canales de calcio
Agentes que actúan sobre el sistema Renina-Angiotensina
Reductores del colesterol y los triglicéridos
Hormonas sexuales y moduladores del sistema genital
Antiinfecciosos para Uso Sistémico
Antibacterianos para uso sistémico
Sistema Musculoesquelético
Antiinflamatorios y antirreumáticos no esteroideos
Sistema Nervioso
Analgésicos
Ansiolíticos
Hipnóticos y sedantes
Antidepresivos
Sistema Respiratorio
Agentes padecimientos obstructivos de vías respiratorias

Ventas de productos farmacéuticos

Ventas farmacéuticas totales
A-Tracto alimentario y metabolismo
B-Sangre y órganos formadores de sangre
C-Sistema cardiovascular

D-Dermatológicos

G-Sistema genitourinario y hormonas sexuales

H-Preparados hormonales sistemas, excluyendo hormonas sexuales/insulinas

J-Antiinfecciosos para uso sistémico

L-Agentes antineoplásicos e inmunomoduladores

M-Sistema musculoesquelético

N-Sistema nervioso

P-Productos antiparasitarios,insecticidas y repelentes

R-Sistema respiratorio

S-Órganos de los sentidos

V-Varios

Otros productos no clasificados

PARTE 8 - DETERMINANTES NO MÉDICOS DE LA SALUD

Modos de vida y comportamientos

Alimentación

Aporte calórico total

Aporte total de proteínas

Consumo de mantequilla

Consumo de azúcar

Consumo de frutas y legumbres

Consumo de alcohol

Consumo de alcohol

Consumo de tabaco

Consumo de tabaco

Peso corporal y composición

Población con sobrepeso

Población obesa

Población con sobrepeso u obesa

Medio ambiente: calidad del aire

Emisiones de óxido de azufre

Emisiones de óxido de nitrógeno

Emisiones de monóxido de carbono

PARTE 9 - REFERENCIAS DEMOGRÁFICAS

Demográficas generales

Población total

Población femenina

Población masculina

Fecundidad

Natalidad

Muerte

Ratio de dependencia de edad

Población por estructura de edad

Población total

Población: 0 a 14 años de edad

Población: 0 a 19 años de edad

Población de 15 años de edad o más

Población: 15 a 49 años de edad

Población: 15 a 64 años de edad

Población: de 20 a 64 años de edad

Población: 65 años de edad o más

Población: 65 a 69 años de edad

Población: 70 a 74 años de edad

Población de 75 a 79 años de edad

Población de 80 años de edad o más

Población activa

Población activa

Empleo total

Población activa total

Empleo asalariado

Empleos a jornada parcial

Desempleo total

Nivel de educación

Nivel de formación ISCED 0/1/2

Nivel de formación ISCED 3/4

Nivel de formación ISCED 5B

Nivel de formación ISCED 5A/6

Esperanza escolar

Gasto total público y privado para instituciones educativas

PARTE 10 - REFERENCIAS ECONÓMICAS

Referencias macro-económicas

Producto interno bruto

Consumo final de las administraciones públicas

Gasto de consumo final de los hogares

Formación bruta de capital fijo

Gasto general de las administraciones públicas

Ingreso público

Remuneraciones de los asalariados
Sueldo medio de obrero de producción
Créditos presupuestos de I+D (total)

Tipo de cambio monetario

Paridad de poder de compra del PIB, US$
Paridad de poder de compra, farmacia, US$
Tipo de cambio del US$

BIBLIOGRAFÍA

Publicaciones recientes de la OCDE en el campo de la salud

HEALTH AT A GLANCE : OECD Indicators 2003 (2003)

SOCIETY AT A GLANCE (2002)
OECD Social indicators, Edition 2002

MEASURING UP: IMPROVING HEALTH SYSTEMS PERFORMANCE IN OECD COUNTRIES (2002)

OECD SOCIAL EXPENDITURE DATABASE, 1980-1998 (2001)
Disponible en inglés y francés en CD-ROM

REFORMS FOR AN AGEING SOCIETY (2000)

A SYSTEM OF HEALTH ACCOUNTS (2000)

Health Working Papers

Une nueva serie para la difusión de estudios sobre la salud, preparados inicialmente para uso dentro de la OCDE. Disponible para su descarga gratuita en: www.oecd.org/els/health/workingpapers.

Los números más recientes son los siguientes:

Health-Care Systems: Lessons from the Reform Experience (OECD Health Working Papers No.9) December 2003

Private Health Insurance in Australia: A Case Study (OECD Health Working Papers No.8) October 2003

Explaining Waiting Times Variations for Elective Surgery across OECD Countries (OECD Health Working Paper No.7) October 2003

Tackling Excessive Waiting Times for Elective Surgery: A Comparison of Policies in Twelve OECD Countries (OECD Health Working Paper No.6) July 2003

Stroke Care in OECD Countries: A Comparison of Treatment, Costs and Outcomes in 17 Countries (OECD Health Working Papers NO.5) June 2003

Survey of Pharmacoeconomic Assessment Activity in Eleven Countries (OECD Health Working Paper NO.4) May 2003

OECD Study of Cross-National Differences in the Treatment, Costs and Outcomes of Ischaemic Heart Disease (OECD Health Working Paper NO.3) April 2003

Investment in Population Health in Five OECD Countries (OECD Health Working Paper N°2) April 2003

Pharmaceutical Use and Expenditure for Cardiovascular Disease and Stroke: a Study of 12 OECD Countries (OECD Health Working Papers No.1) February 2003

Documentos ocasionales de politica social relacionados con la salud

Disponible para su descarga gratuita sobre http://www.oecd.org/document/25/0,2340,en_2649_33929_2380441_1_1_1_1,00.html.

Los números más recientes son los siguientes:

No. 57 IMPROVING THE PERFORMANCE OF HEALTH CARE SYSTEMS: FROM MEASURES TO ACTION (2001) Zeynep Or

No. 56 AN ASSESSMENT OF THE PERFORMANCE OF THE JAPANESE HEALTH CARE SYSTEM (2001) Hyoung-Sun Jeong y Jeremy Hurst

No. 53 TOWARDS MORE CHOICE IN SOCIAL PROTECTION? INDIVIDUAL CHOICE OF INSURER IN BASIC MANDATORY HEALTH INSURANCE IN SWITZERLAND (2001) Francesca Colombo

No. 47 PERFORMANCE MEASUREMENT AND PERFORMANCE MANAGEMENT IN OECD HEALTH SYSTEMS (2001) Jeremy Hurst y Melissa Jee-Hughes

Puede obtener la lista completa de las publicaciones de la OCDE en el sitio Internet de su libreria:
www.oecd.org/bookshop
o escribiendo a la dirección siguiente, especificando que desea recibirgratuitamente
el catálogo de publicaciones de la OCDE:
Service des Publications OCDE
2, rue André-Pascal, 75775 PARIS CEDEX 16

Español